Guard the Chaos

Guard the Chaos

Finding meaning in change

Hannah Ward and Jennifer Wild

DARTON · LONGMAN + TODD

First published 1995 by
Darton, Longman and Todd Ltd
1 Spencer Court
140–142 Wandsworth High Street
London SW18 4JJ

ISBN 0–232–52049–6

A catalogue record for this book is available
from the British Library.

Acknowledgement
The extracts from *Collected Poems* by Edwin Muir,
published by Faber and Faber Ltd, are reproduced
by permission.

Photypeset by Intype, London

Printed and bound in Great Britain
at the University Press, Cambridge

*For our families
and friends:*

the Womenspace women
with whom we explore the things that matter;

other women in England and New Zealand
who contributed their ideas in our workshops;

Tim Russ and Martin Courts
who lent us their house and cats
at this book's eleventh hour;

Mary Jean Pritchard
midwife of this book
and mother of our god-daughter Anna;

the Community of St Clare at Freeland
who offer us generous friendship
and their library;

Pen Eckersley
in whose house we have found a home
and stimulating company;

Jennifer's family
for continuing to be, however distantly, there;

Chris and Bill Ward, Hannah's parents
providers of a much loved bolt hole by the sea,
whose life together through the last year
before Bill died as we finished this book,
gave us an inspiring example of coping with one of
life's most fundamental changes.

Contents

Introduction

Whether it is adapting to the presence of women priests, no longer finding beliefs in virgin birth and bodily resurrection tenable, or finding the language of the liturgy intolerably sexist, many of us no longer feel entirely at home in our church. The churches themselves are being shaken into chaos by financial crises, by lay members discovering that they really *are* their own theologians, and by ordained clergy declaring themselves in ways not entirely consistent with official church teaching.

Is all this the beginning of the end of Christianity, or could it be the work of the Holy Spirit?

We see these events rather as signs of the times – changing times – in which we can read ends and beginnings, threats and promises, destruction and creation. Indeed, we are facing the same need to live creatively with change in our 'religious' journey as in many other areas of life. Why should we expect it to be otherwise? God, the same yesterday, today and for ever? Yes – but not our images of God, nor the vehicles through which we express our experience of God; not even the religion we construct in order to 'contain' God.

One of the things we shall be looking at in this book is the way in which the process of change reveals the 'nature of things' – of institutions, people, ideas. Definitions are not as clear-cut as we would sometimes like to think they are. A boundary separating inside from outside is no fine line, but resembles a gap that must be traversed with care, that can provide at least a temporary home, and that is full of creative potential as well as threatened disintegration and breakdown. Those who find themselves on or near the boundary – those we call 'boundary-dwellers' – are not necessarily 'marginal' but rather are on a threshold, signifying the end of something old, the beginning of something new.

> The border is there to dislodge you from previous attachments, a symbol of estrangement and initiation. And at the border we are exposed to two conflicting pulls; we want to stay behind but we are also prompted to leave and to arrive.[1]

This book attempts to map the experience of being 'betwixt and between' – in a state of chaos, being neither one thing nor another. Why? At first glance it would appear that, on a personal level, such experiences are entirely negative. For example, the process of struggling with an important decision when the right course of action is far from clear; the sudden loss of security and status when facing redundancy; the shock of being told that one's illness is life-threatening: these are all situations in which we experience a familiar world crumbling with no sign of a new world to take its place. They are all times of 'betwixt and between' when we find ourselves in the middle, between what has been and what is yet to be.

And yet we find in different religions that this time and experience is given a particularly sacred quality. The anthropologist Arnold van Gennep describes it as the 'liminal', from the Latin word *limen* meaning 'threshold'. He shows in his writings how the liminal period of any rite of passage, such as an initiation rite at puberty, is its most sacred and intense moment.

We learn, too, from the great Tibetan Buddhist tradition that the 'bardo' state of the death process, the betwixt-and-between time between death and rebirth, offers the disciple the greatest potential moment for enlightenment.

In the Christian tradition there is much about wilderness, understood as times and places of testing, of purification, of God's presence as well as God's absence; indeed, the whole Christian era is seen as between one coming and a Second Coming. The Christian is exhorted to live as one in transit, taking no thought for the morrow, storing up no treasure on earth, losing life in order to find it.

Consider again those major decisions we have made in our own lives. Do we not find some truth in the words of W. H. Auden that 'the distresses of choice are our chance to be blessed'; that the in-between time, the time of not knowing, can offer new insights that lead to our growth as human beings? Similarly, people who know they are soon to die can sometimes experience a deep inner healing that would otherwise not have occurred.

In the experience of many contemporary Christians there is a real sense of wilderness, a sense of having grown out of, or away from, old belief systems and forms of worship. We experience the present as barren and bewildering; the old has died but the new is beyond our grasp. How do those of us who dwell uneasily on the boundaries of the institutional churches, and perhaps of Christianity itself, live there creatively both for ourselves and for the wider Christian community?

A central argument of this book is that Christians who tend to express their faith outside or on the fringes of the institutional churches are not necessarily a bunch of unfaithful doubters whom the churches should tolerate or regard as a pastoral problem. Rather they are Christians called into the wilderness to find new ways of being church, forming faith communities with their own theological and liturgical life and with much to offer the 'mainstream' churches. Creating new ways of being church is necessary because of the need we all have of a container for our religious faith and its expression. For many, the historical churches have ceased to offer an appropriately shaped container. We just do not fit. To be true to ourselves and to God we have to move out, at least part time. And there is a moving out that is not a leaving for a marginal, much less for a sectarian, existence. We claim there is a challenge both for those on the move and those left behind to see the movers as still a live part of the community of faith, indeed of their own denomination where they retain such membership.

One characteristic of this liminal state is a sense of ambivalence: we are not really sure whether we are in or out of the church, or, more often, we feel we are both in and out. The truth in our experience concerns the nature of boundaries – the existence of that whole grey area between one side and another. It makes those who order religious institutions twitch at the thought, but it is a place where things happen and where the creative spirit of God has a bit of elbow room. We call it the wilderness.

If we are to make dwelling in such a place a creative experience, we need first to understand the nature of the wilderness in which we find ourselves. In search of such understanding we shall revisit the Bible and some elements in Christian tradition, and consider some findings of psychology and social anthropology. We shall be using the word 'liminal' to describe wilderness experience as denoting an in-between time – the time of travelling, of having left but not yet arrived.

Chapters 6, 7 and 8 of the book focus on our own wilderness community – that of Christian feminists and other Christian women who find no comfortable place, or no place at all, in a patriarchal church. Although addressed primarily to that community, many of the practical questions raised by the ambivalence of being ill at ease with mainstream Christianity will echo those of other individuals and groups on a similar journey. What we hope to stress is that the wilderness journey inevitably involves exodus, which in turn implies loss and the need for appropriate grieving. We offer some suggestions as to how this can be managed.

How we survive in the wilderness and how we live there creatively are important questions because in a sense the betwixt-and-between experiences we have pointed to focus a much more general experience of our time. We live in a world today where many old certainties have disappeared and much that we took for granted no longer withstands contemporary doubt and questioning. The end of 1989 demonstrated with forceful clarity the in-between state which followed the end of communist rule in much of Eastern Europe and which precedes the establishment of any new political system.

So we return to the question, how do we experience times of betwixt and between as blessed and full of creative potential rather than disintegrative and paralysing? How do we begin to save ourselves from nostalgia for the past and terror for the future? We don't know, but we have a hunch that the everyday experiences of being betwixt and between that we started with hold some secret for us. For at the heart of those experiences is both a call and a need to 'guard the chaos'. They present us with the challenge to guard or protect the creative potential in change *and* to guard or contain the accompanying threat of disintegration.

Any religious tradition, to be tenable in the present age, needs to have something to say to us about these experiences that helps us to make sense of them and live through them creatively. A retreat into the certainties of fundamentalism has already shown its cost. We must search hard for a spirituality that embraces change rather than denies it. That search is what this book is about.

1

All Change[1]

We live in a world of change. We live with changing ideas, changing moral norms, changing world politics, changing boundaries in outer space, changing definitions of what it means to be alive. 'Change' has become a major item on the human agenda. The amount of change in our modern world means that books and courses on the subject are often entitled 'How to *cope* with change'. Institutions typically learn to 'manage change'. Rarely do we see workshops on 'The joy of change'! There is a vast array of literature about change, from the perspectives of a wide range of disciplines. Change is big business.

We went looking for a psychological map of change and found lots of maps, each too complex for us to attempt to describe here in any detail. But even a fairly quick glance at some of the theories and models on offer indicates that they agree about at least two things: first, change is a *process* and it is possible to define stages or phases within that process; second, the experience of change is an ambivalent one, potentially creative and destructive. These things hold true whether the change is personal or social.

There are various attempts also to classify types of change and transitions in our lives. There are changes in important roles: for example, ceasing studies as a student and becoming a teacher; separating or divorcing from a marriage partner;

becoming a parent. There are changes concerning a person's environment: moving house; emigrating to another country. And there are physiological changes: losing the ability to see or hear; having a limb amputated; coming to terms with a life-threatening illness. Still other changes have to do with life-stages and the aging process.

This is by no means an exhaustive list. There are other kinds of change to deal with: new knowledge that might affect our previously held moral beliefs and attitudes; a significant new experience triggered by new technology that might deeply affect the way we see the world. Modern communications technology means that the sheer volume of new information and ideas we are faced with constantly challenges us to change: to rethink, to accommodate, to leave behind, to move on.

Just as experiences of change are different, so will reactions be different. Psychologists and sociologists use words like 'adaptation', 'mastery', 'coping', and 'defence' to describe responses to change. Who we are, whom we have around us, what our previous experience has been – as well as the nature of the change we face – are just some of the factors which will influence how we cope with (or celebrate) change.

One of the main reasons why change tends to be viewed negatively is that it causes stress. Just after Hannah left a religious order after nearly nine years, she was given a book which included a well-known table of the causes of stress. Top of the list is the death of a spouse, with other family deaths, redundancy, moving house, holidays and the Christmas period appearing further down the list. Each event is given a number of points; add up those points for the events which have been part of your life over the last year and you measure the likelihood of your having a serious illness in the next year. (Hannah made it reasonably healthily through her next year despite an estimated eighty per cent chance of illness!)

Change can be experienced as crisis, particularly if we have been very quickly propelled into a major life change by something beyond our control. At such times we not only need the support of our friends, family and work colleagues, but may also need counselling or some other form of professional help.

Crisis therapy has been developed by a number of people in the world of psychiatry, among them Gerald Caplan.[2] Caplan's theory is based on the concept of *emotional homeostasis*. Life for none of us is constantly straightforward and calm; we frequently meet all kinds of hazards which upset our emotional balance. These hazards do not usually constitute any major threat to our equilibrium as we can overcome them with previously learned skills. Sometimes, however, the hazard is bigger and more complicated than we have met before, or it is one that surprises us by its sheer unfamiliarity. In such a circumstance we are thrown emotionally (and perhaps physically) off balance and experience crisis.

Caplan's crisis therapy developed with the recognition that this temporary crisis state 'of heightened susceptibility can present unparalleled opportunities for internal boundary realignment, for better or for worse'.[3] In other words, the shifting of external boundaries involved in sudden change which causes us to experience a crisis, forces the temporary loss of internal psychological boundaries. As a result of this we are faced with both the opportunity for personal growth and the danger of long-term psychological damage. In Caplan's words:

> A crisis is provoked when a person faces an obstacle to important life goals that is, for a time, insurmountable through the utilisation of customary methods of problem-solving. A period of disorganisation ensues, a period of upset, during which many different abortive attempts at solution are made. Eventually some kind of adaptation is achieved, which may or may not be in the best interests of that person and his [*sic*] fellows.[4]

In other words, the experience of crisis feels in part as if someone has suddenly snatched the rug from under our feet. We are thrown off balance; we are at sea; we lose much of the sense of who we are. At these times, if the experience of crisis is to lead to growth, we need to be 'held' firmly by those close to us – family, friends, colleagues, therapist. The longer the crisis is prolonged, the more danger there is of the person in crisis 'falling apart'.

This all sounds a bit dramatic for a chapter about 'ordinary' experiences of change. And what has it got to do with 'the wilderness'?

Before you read any further, take a few moments to try this experiment: reflect on your experience of one major change in your life. It does not matter what the particular change was; recognise it first as a *process*; reflect on the process of the change and picture the shape of that process. You might like to draw it. Try to remember what sort of feelings accompanied each phase of that process of change.

This is a good exercise to illustrate that change does not happen overnight. We know that, of course, but it is extraordinary how often we forget it. We expect to be able to make even quite major changes in our lives without too much trouble and we are sometimes rather taken aback when we feel 'thrown' by change. We might give ourselves (generously, we think) three months to 'get over' some major change, and are alarmed to find it takes three years. It is all the more disturbing when we have deliberately chosen the change.

Despite knowing that we live in a fast-changing world, and to some extent being used to change, we still find personal change in our own lives very difficult. We fear it and so try to avoid it; we deny the need for it. 'Better the devil we know' are often the words of our inner voice. Major changes in our lives all mean upheaval. More often than not, as we have seen, change is something we have to face whether we like it or not: we are made redundant; a flatmate leaves to get married; we learn we have a life-threatening illness; our partner dies. These examples may again seem rather dramatic, but many of the same uncomfortable feelings accompany any difficult decision involving change. For it is rarely the case that an important decision is made in an instant, or even overnight. Rather, we engage in a process of decision-making, that phrase itself implying a lengthy and laborious task of deciding. Such a process is often painful and we describe ourselves as agonising over the decision. What in fact we are often describing is the state of not knowing. This is a kind of in-between time when we know a decision has to be made, but it is not actually made. We are in the position of knowing what is not or what has been, without knowing what is or is to be. At such times we are tempted to decide prematurely and find ourselves in the wrong place, or the wrong job, because we cannot stand the chaos of being unable to decide. We have too many options, or not enough, or may be too fearful of letting go of what we already have. Sometimes it is because we cannot live with the voice inside saying, 'I don't know, I just don't know'. All these may be the case, yet we still instinctively know that staying in this chaotic in-between place, the place of boundary, is a vital part of the process. This is where the real discernment takes place, where we have to listen to ourselves and look at our life to discover which move or which change will take us that bit closer to our own truth and its living.

The word 'boundary' is central to the subject and argument of this book. When we experience change, we experience boundary. Boundaries are about change – or the lack of it. They may be rigid or flexible. We may find them liberating or stifling. They may drive us out of our minds, or they may save our sanity. We have said this book is especially for 'boundary-dwellers', so it is important that we look more closely at what we are saying about the nature of boundaries.

To offer a simple image: in the days when you went by sea rather than by air, Jennifer left New Zealand, bound for an unknown length of stay in England. The decision to go did not take place overnight. That decision had its own largely hidden process. The process of the move from Wellington to Cambridge is more obvious. First, there is a good deal of practical and emotional preparation: packing, buying tickets, preparing to leave family and friends. Then there is the actual leaving and saying goodbye. But the unpacking and the beginning of new friendships doesn't happen for another five weeks or so. For those five weeks are spent literally at sea. If someone had asked Jennifer during week three, say, where she was, she would probably not have answered in terms of a particular bit of ocean, but with something like 'on my way to England'. For when we are in the middle of a move we are aware not so much of the immediate present but of the past and future. We have left and we will arrive; for the present, we are in a state of limbo – we are *in between*, we are on the extended boundary between where we have been and where we will be. In Jennifer's case, the five weeks at sea represented that boundary.

What is that experience like? Again, in Jennifer's case, we might have an image of her sitting blissfully in a deck chair sunning herself, just waiting for England to appear on the horizon. But probably, even if in a deck chair, she was making all kinds of psychological adjustments: for example, coming to terms with the loss of having her family around; 'psyching herself up' to make new friends and begin a new life in Cambridge. She may have also spent time doing practical things concerning the move: writing to the friends she had left behind; reading about aspects of life in England.

This is, as we said, a visual and simplified example, and one of a change that was chosen. But the shape of the process is probably similar in most cases of change (think back to your own example earlier). There is a phase leading up to something happening, or a sudden event (like an accidental death), followed by a period of chaos or waiting when the change is happening but not complete, and finally a new and relatively stable life situation. Remember, this may be a major change (bereavement or redundancy) or one that is chosen (a holiday, for example, where the holiday week itself is the in-between time).

The language we commonly use today about our religious faith betrays this same atmosphere of change. We are 'pilgrims' on a 'journey of faith', we live a 'life of faith' rather than assent to a set of beliefs. The journey of faith has its own moments of radical change where the overwhelming sense is one of 'destination unknown'.

The change is once again personal and social. On a personal level, many Christians (and others) have been forced to rethink long-cherished beliefs about, for example, the virgin birth, bodily resurrection or papal infallibility, because of new scholarship, general social trends, Vatican II and so on. A high degree of social mobility where people may move several times in a lifetime from one area to another may mean leaving a parish after years of worshipping there. A new vicar may bring a whole new flavour to a church, leading to some members feeling forced out.

On a corporate, institutional level the obvious example of significant change in England as we write this is the Church of England's decision to ordain women to the priesthood. Before we reflect on that, however, we want to look further at one of the most important aspects of change – loss.

Loss and change

To move is to leave. To change is to lose. Every time we choose, we say no to something.

Moving, changing and choosing are all things we are generally encouraged to view positively. The alternative is the proverbial rut. Yet very often we do not take the task of moving, changing and choosing anything like seriously enough. We expect it to have its difficult moments, but we tend not to prepare ourselves nor do we allow ourselves to enter fully into the process. Why?

It has much to do with the denial of death that is prevalent in western cultures. We live with fairly constant television pictures of people starving or massacred in Africa, war-torn in Bosnia, or, until recently, murdered in Northern Ireland, but we are generally unable to confront death, live with death, when it is close at hand.

In hospital culture, death is an embarrassment and a

reminder of 'failure' to the medical profession. Everything surrounding death tends to be carried out quickly and 'efficiently'; the doctor, the undertaker, the crematorium, often even the priest, all seem to conspire to make death – a dead body – as invisible as possible. The pressure is on for a quick burial so that *life* can get swiftly back to normal.

This denial of death, and the chaos of feeling that death brings, reflects a much wider denial of loss in western cultures. One area where we see this is in the workplace. Gerald Arbuckle cites the work of William Lutz in this connection:

> The covering up of loss throughout society in general has become a sad form of art. William Lutz recently invented the term 'doublespeak' to describe this corruption of language; the word connotes a very conscious use of language as a weapon or tool by those in power to achieve their ends at the expense of others. Through doublespeak, those who are powerful aim to hide for their advantage the reality of pain and loss in all areas of life. People who are sacked, in doublespeak are 'dehired' or 'selected out' by firms that are having 'workforce adjustments'; when Chrysler closed a plant, it 'initiated a career alternative enhancement program' and some 5,000 employees lost their jobs.[5]

Just as someone's dying is referred to as their 'passing away', so bosses tell employees 'I'm afraid I'm going to have to let you go'. Perhaps worse still is the way in which employment change is sometimes managed. For example, an executive sees her own job advertised in a national newspaper before anything has been said to her; or a manager returns from holiday to discover someone else's name on his door and a stranger at his desk. Both of these are examples from real life.

There are also consultants who specialise in helping companies manage their staff changes, supposedly as painlessly as possible for all concerned. Their great claim is that they can clear an employee and all his or her possessions out of an office and away from the building within half an hour, without the company even having to pay the taxi fare. This must surely represent a denial of loss for the employee and for his or her colleagues. So why do it?

What is happening here (and in our denial of physical death) is an attempt to skip the in-between stage of change, the stage that is full of chaos and tension for all concerned. Writers on grieving and mourning may disagree about the names and numbers of stages in the grieving process, but they do agree that it is a *process*, and that its movement is complex. Any definition of the stages is therefore necessarily over-simplified and generalised. Also, grief is experienced not just by individuals, but by groups, nations and cultures. Just as individuals try to deny the chaotic in-between stage of the grieving process, so do whole cultures and groups of all sizes.

Broadly speaking there are three stages (or groups of stages) in the grieving process. Whatever names they are given, they indicate a movement from knowing who and where we are, through the chaos of disorientation caused by loss, to a state of recovery where we regain some sense of balance and relative security.

The first stage is one of shock and is marked by sadness and a reluctance to face the loss. It can move into a time of denial when we try to repress or project our feelings on to those close to us or those whom we blame for our loss.

The second stage is one of disorientation, a chaotic time full of tensions. It is a time of confusion for the bereaved and often a time when it is not possible to get on with usual day-to-day activities. C. S. Lewis captures this quality in *A Grief Observed*:

And grief still feels like fear. Perhaps, more strictly, like suspense. Or like waiting; just hanging about waiting for something to happen. It gives life a permanently provisional feeling. It doesn't seem worth starting anything. I can't settle down. I yawn, I fidget, I smoke too much. Up till this I always had too little time. Now there is

nothing but time. Almost pure time, empty success-
iveness.[6]

Gerald Arbuckle also gives some good examples of what
can happen at this stage when the grieving process is a social/
cultural one. In this second stage:

> a culture feels both attracted by the security of the past
> and the call to face the future. It is a period of sometimes
> anxious reflection, a search into mythological roots to
> obtain a sense of identity and self-worth. This can lead
> to outbursts of localized excessive nationalism or delusions
> of grandeur, a widespread repression or denial of the
> realities of loss. This is a risky time because the temptation
> is for the culture or organization to cling tenaciously to
> what has been lost and simply refuse to face the future;
> the group can initiate a spectacular project that is totally
> out of touch with reality [one can't help thinking of
> the churches' Decade of Evangelism/Evangelization]. For
> example, a Third World country in the midst of economic
> and social chaos starts its own international airline to give
> itself the feeling that 'we are as good as anyone else', or a
> parish that is in grave financial debt decides to refurbish
> the church 'to make parishioners feel good'. If these resis-
> tances to reality continue, chronic grief takes over and it
> is extremely difficult, if not impossible, for a culture to
> move out of the escapist depression. People may then
> come 'to love being miserable' and this gives the particular
> culture its warped sense of identity or belonging; on the
> other hand, people can become so feverishly busy that
> the pain of loss is repressed.[7]

The third and final stage in the grieving process represents
a kind of recovery of balance in which life can go on anew,
the past not denied but incorporated into the future.

This whole process may take a very long time indeed. The
important point about it is that there can be no short-cuts.
Roger Grainger writes:

For the new situation to 'live', the old one must 'die'. Thus there is always a crucial point 'between', a point representing the condition after the old state of affairs has come to an end and before the new one has actually begun. This is the moment of real change, the pivotal moment that has no movement of itself, but permits movement to take place.[8]

Paul Ricoeur also offers us a three-stage model of change which helps us understand the importance of this in-between phase.[9] His terms are *orientation*, *disorientation* and *reorientation*. In the orientation stage we have a sense of identity; then something happens which propels us into the period of disorientation. A central characteristic of this time is the tension between, on the one hand, 'the movement to cling to what has been lost as a source of a much needed sense of belonging', and, on the other hand, 'the ability to go out and grasp a revitalized identity in a new world'.[10] The stronger of these pulls in the stage of disorientation will be the pull of the past, a nostalgic longing for things as they were. Once the movement to newness and the future begins to be stronger, the individual or group begins to enter the third stage of reorientation when a new identity becomes established.

It is worth repeating here that for a new identity and a future that incorporates the past, the grieving process must be entered into in all its stages. Most significantly, there can be no leap from stage one to stage three, from the moment of shock/crisis/loss to a new future. Such a leap is exactly the lie that the western denial of death and loss perpetuates. A quick funeral, clearing out the dead person's possessions as soon as possible, plunging into new activities – none of these can take the place of a time of utter disorientation in the grieving process.

Likewise, in our other example, not only the redundant employee, but also his or her colleagues and the company as a whole, will suffer from being denied the time to live

with and through the loss and chaos that change brings
with it.

Once again, we may expect this to be true of unpleasant
changes, like death or redundancy or divorce. But it is also
true of changes we choose, and, often very painfully, of
changes we are supposed to be thrilled about. How many
mothers, for example, do not experience a sense of chaos
and loss after the birth of a baby (especially if it is their
first)? Motherhood and fatherhood are utterly romanticised,
both in the advertisements we are bombarded with and in
the strong denial that parents should ever feel (never mind
express) dark and negative emotions towards their newly
born offspring. But how could everything possibly always be
sweetness and light? A relationship between two people has
been radically disrupted; a house or flat that felt quite
spacious for two is suddenly cluttered, cramped and chaotic;
the lack of sleep and sheer physical exhaustion of it all makes
coping with the rest of life barely possible; and, particularly
for the mother, there may well be a radical change of identity
from a career-defined identity to motherhood. Never mind
a friend giving the parents a break to go shopping: they
might have more need of a space to sit down and howl.

The churches on the whole are not very good at dealing
with loss, except perhaps physical death. Apart from the
funeral service there are very few services on offer which
mark endings. There is a rite of passage for marriage, but
not for separation or divorce. There are services of welcome
and commitment for those who join religious orders, but
nothing to mark a person's leaving. There are services of
installation and enthronement for clergy and bishops taking
up new appointments; but have you ever been to a service
of 'dethronement'?

The way we say our public goodbyes to people in these
and other work situations is usually with a party. It is hard
to express very much grief at a party where, even if loss is
mentioned, we are still supposed to 'have a good time'. Still
more significantly, we have not seen in any of the British
churches' prayer books a service to mark retirement, despite

its being one of the most significant moments in a person's life.[11]

It is of course not true that there are *no* leaving rituals for the sorts of occasions we have just mentioned. Social workers sometimes provide separation rituals for those divorcing, and such rituals are becoming much more common in the USA; and the new Anglican Franciscan office book contains a service entitled 'Praying our Farewells'. This service does not, however, appear to acknowledge or express the loss for the community as a whole, only that of the person departing: the group does not appear to see itself changing with the loss of a member.

The problem with change is that we cannot celebrate and live the new without moving from and letting go of the old. And the new does not usually arrive or fall into place at the very same moment when we are asked to leave the old. Change is a process. At the centre of this process lies the inevitable experience of chaos: sometimes so minor it is imperceptible; at other times its force threatens to overwhelm entirely. The chaos is both outer and inner. The outer chaos has to do with things being in flux. At the time of writing this chapter we are living between two houses. We are in the process of moving from the bottom of a house to the top, and are spending fourteen hours a day for three months in another house half a mile away. We have toothbrushes in both places, and books and papers constantly in the 'wrong' place. It is chaos.

Inner chaos has to do with identity. Arbuckle cites a basic anthropological fact of life: 'we yearn for a sense of identity and belonging and we dread chaos, its enemy. Once we have this gift of identity . . . we do everything we can to avoid losing it; if we do lose this identity, we often deny that it has been destroyed.'[12] Some loss of identity occurs in many cases of change. For example, the loss of identity as wife when a woman separates from her husband; the loss of identity as 'the vicar' when a man or woman leaves parish ministry; the loss of identity as, say, chemist or teacher when a person retires.

What is particularly hard is the time immediately following the first stage of change – the chaotic in-between time before any new identity is established. This is as true for societies as for individuals and we have already cited the social upheaval of Eastern Europe as an example. There is good reason to fear the loss of identity and to feel ambivalent about even the changes we choose. But we *do* choose to change, even when we know in advance that we are in for a rough ride in the weeks, months or even years to come. At such moments we take our life into our hands and move because we know that to stay still would be to deny the potential for things like truth, personal or social maturity, justice, and so on.

It is important for us to note the two inseparable elements in any crisis: danger and opportunity. Indeed, the Chinese symbol for crisis is formed by the pictographs for danger and opportunity. We find these two elements cropping up again and again as central characteristics in any understanding of change, whether it be personal or social. They appear to be related to the experience of a 'gap' that must be negotiated wherever a significant boundary has to be crossed.

The experience of 'gap' is most notably acknowledged in the Tibetan Buddhist concept of the Great Bardo and in the reading of the Book of the Dead. 'Bardo' means 'gap' and the Great Bardo is that time and place between death and rebirth. It is full of dangers and temptations which prevent a person letting go. The Book of the Dead is read as a guide, for the Great Bardo also represents the most intense opportunity for awakening. All the little bardo experiences which happen in life provide the person with opportunities to practise.

Another important element in the Buddhist training and preparation for death is how, through contemplation as well as meditation, the individual works towards an emotional acceptance of death, and learns how to make use of the crises, upheavals and changes of life. These changes or small deaths that occur so frequently in our lives are a living link with death, prompting us to let go and revealing the possibility of seeing, in the gap they open up, the sky-like, empty, open space of the true nature of our mind. *In the transition and uncertainty of change lies the opportunity for awakening.* [our italics][13]

The next few chapters will explore the meaning and significance of the wilderness as 'gap' and place of transition.

2
Sacred and Dangerous

In the previous chapter we have concentrated on individual change. We have seen how change can mean crisis, and looked at the psychological 'map' of a major life change for a person.

But what of the religious map, the spiritual map, that attempts to make sense of and give meaning to such profound changes? Does the language of religion add anything to our understanding of these experiences? Does it offer more than 'comfortable words' which crumble when put to the test? Does that part of ourselves which we speak of as 'spiritual' or 'spiritual life' face similar unsettling change?

We shall be turning to social anthropologists to help answer some of these questions. We have found in their work a model for change which seems to offer something creative to our understanding of change. We do not want to suggest a wholly uncritical approach to this model, but would invite the reader to use and explore it with openness and without necessarily accepting other aspects of particular studies of, for example, initiation rites.

Fundamentally, we are still concerned with change: what is its shape and how can it be managed so that it is creative rather than destructive? In this chapter we shall be concerned particularly with the social aspects of change, that is, how it affects the wider group.

The most important concept we want to introduce is that of *liminality*. Liminality is what this book is essentially about – the concept that we find makes most sense of and gives most meaning to all kinds of seemingly negative and uncomfortable experiences in life.

The term 'liminality' was first used by Arnold van Gennep, a French anthropologist whose famous book *Rites de Passage* was published in 1909.[1] The concept has been further developed by other anthropologists, most notably Victor and Edith Turner.[2] Liminality can be described as 'an ambiguous, sacred, social state in which a person or group of persons is separated for a time from the normal structure of society'.[3] This implies, of course, that societies have structures. We can see various kinds of structure. First, people are given and take on for themselves all sorts of roles and functions: some clearly defined, others less so. Within different roles we operate in different spheres of society: the doctor in a hospital or general practice; the cashier in a branch of Tesco; the council landscape gardener in a local park; and so on.

Second, we are aware of hierarchical structure: the managing director has his coffee brought into his office; the head-mistress detains a wayward pupil after school; a back-bench MP makes a televised statement supporting the Prime Minister's controversial new policy.

Finally, and probably most important, there are whole sets of much less clear 'rules': underlying assumptions about how we ought to behave in certain circumstances. These might be age-old customs or recently arrived-at expectations. We are aware of them sometimes only when we break them. This underlying structural logic gives social life an order and a predictability. When it is undisturbed people and objects 'fit' – they are in the right place at the right time, in the right way.

What interests us here, however, is what happens when the rules are broken or the established social order is disrupted. Suppose one morning out of the blue the managing director makes everybody else's cups of coffee and brings them to their offices. At the very least, we would wonder what the special occasion was. And if he insisted on doing this regularly, many employees would feel positively uncomfortable. And how would you feel if as soon as you entered your new GP's surgery she started pouring out all her personal problems? What would your reaction be if the supermarket cashier looked at your trolley and suggested you come back to the check-out when you had chosen a healthier selection of groceries for your family?

In each case, feelings of discomfort or anger arise because things, or rather people, are not as they should be; underlying assumptions about behaviour have not been fulfilled. This is one way in which the normal social pattern is thrown or at least threatened. But social patterns are also threatened when less strange changes occur. For example, when a parent is admitted to hospital, even if for only a relatively short stay, a number of people are affected: mum/dad can't meet the children from school; there is no partner to help share chores; work colleagues need to cover urgent jobs; teachers may have to deal with anxious young children. Especially if it is a prolonged hospital stay, a whole pattern of relationships will need to change. The normal running of things – like the family – will be suspended during this time. For the person in hospital particularly, but also for others closely affected, this is a *liminal* time: they are temporarily separated from the normal structure of society.

This is a kind of enforced liminality, but there are other people who choose a separation. One example would be members of the peace camp established during the Gulf War. This is a good example for demonstrating a central characteristic of the liminal position – that of *ambiguity*. We do not know how to relate to the person who is liminal: they collect both our fears and our awe; there is a certain mystique which surrounds them. This was certainly true of that peace camp. Its fame spread around the world: its members were heroes who focused so much hope and aspiration. They were, at the same time, hated and despised; accused of being insane, traitors, irresponsible parents (and grandparents).

Either way, their action was unusually powerful, a power due in large part to their existence *between* the structures of society. In so being, they lived as prophets have always lived.

Using the word 'between' to describe the position of people who have stepped out of the normal social structure points us to another central characteristic of liminality: it is the place and time of the in-between. Here is where the anthropologists help us understand the ambivalent experience of change.

As we have seen in the previous chapter, change does not happen suddenly – it is usually a process of longer or shorter duration. Change is something we pass through rather than a fine line we quickly and neatly cross. And the process does not necessarily end when the change has been made – we can 'feel the effects' of change for some time. This feeling can be all the more unsettling if we are not sure quite when the change has occurred. One way of making it clearer is through ritual, whether the formal ritual of, say, marriage, or the informal ritual of an office retirement party for a colleague. In their own way, these are *rites of passage*.

Van Gennep defined rites of passage as 'rites which accompany every change of place, state, social position and age'. In other words, rites of passage mark times when the structural pattern of society is 'rattled' by movement. Rites of passage give us a language to express and manage change. The rite is an expression of and for the individual (or group) making the change *and* also for those who will feel or notice its effects, or who will need to know that a new way of relating to the changed individual will now be appropriate.

So there are two key functions of rites of passage: they make a public statement and they 'manage' change by giving it a definition and shape. This latter function is very important. As we saw in the last chapter, change can mean psychological crisis. Crisis can be creative but only for a limited period of time and then only if the individual or group in crisis is held and contained – by family, friends, medical services, neighbours. A rite of passage contains and gives a sense of boundary because it announces when and where change is taking, or has taken, place.

Because change is a process, not instant, rites of passage have phases. Van Gennep, in his study of small-scale societies, distinguished three phases which mark all rites of transition. He describes them as *separation*, *margin* (or *limen*), and *aggregation*. This is perhaps best understood if we look at an initiation rite. If we think in terms of ritual as a language, the rite of separation makes the statement that this person is no longer a child, no longer in the social state called 'childhood'. It is no longer appropriate to relate to her or him as a child or to expect her or him to behave like a child.

The third and final phase of the initiation rite, described as 'aggregation', makes a statement about the new status of the individual; she or he is incorporated back into the social group as an adult member. The new status is celebrated and affirmed in the rite, the passage is complete, and once again everyone knows where they stand.

But what of the middle phase – the margin or, as van Gennep termed it, the liminal phase? The subject of the initiation rite is in a very ambiguous time and place: she or he is no longer a child, but not yet an adult. The person is outside, or more accurately *between*, the structures of society. As such they have no identity; in a sense, they do not exist, at least not as far as their social group is concerned. This is reflected in the way initiands are treated during this phase of the rite. In some societies male initiands will be placed physically outside the community, having to survive for some days, for example, in the bush on the outskirts of the village. Others are buried in mock graves which symbolise the 'death' of their former state in life. Perhaps less dramatic, but still symbolically powerful, is the wearing of masks during this time. This is another way of showing that the liminal person has no identity within the social group.

No wonder, then, that change can be so scary for us all: change threatens our identity *and* it threatens our patterns of relationships, what we might call 'the social order'. We are thrown off balance because things turn out to be less predictable than we thought they were, less secure than we want them to be.

One of the most obvious examples of our awareness of these kinds of feelings is when a friend or a member of our family dies. Especially if it is an unexpected death, we may find ourselves in a state of shock which is not just about our sense of loss but also about a deep feeling of insecurity at how suddenly things can change. 'My world has been shattered' is a phrase that describes this experience all too well. We also find it hard to know how to relate to a bereaved person. They often speak of the pain of being treated like a leper – someone others avoid meeting in the street because of embarrassment at not knowing what to say. This is especially the case between the death and the funeral. The funeral marks, in a way, the return to 'normal' life – often the beginning of bereavement not the end, for until now it is as if the clock had stopped and all life were suspended. The process has been and is one of profound change; one person has died, others have been left without a partner, friend, child, parent, colleague. The time between the death and the funeral is an intensely liminal one – a time between one pattern of relationships and the announcement through the public ritual of the funeral of another one. The funeral not only allows us open expression of our grief, it also lets us know where we stand, however painful the place.

Funerals are rites of transition and will have within them the three phases described by van Gennep. But the phases are also present in the whole process. If we imagine the death of a woman's husband, we could say that the death itself marks the phase of separation: it makes the statement that the woman is no longer a wife in partnership with a husband. The funeral represents the phase of 'aggregation': it makes the statement that the person is dead and by so doing announces the new state of the woman as a widow. The time between death and the funeral is the limen, the threshold between one state and another. To be there is to live with the lack of identity and security which characterises to one degree or another all liminal experiences. The longer this in-between state lasts – because of the need for a post-mortem or the lack of confirmation of death due to a missing body, for example – the more stressful it is for the bereaved and those around them.

Of course, that is to over-simplify and to generalise, but we believe it illustrates that it is not just formal rituals that contain the three phases of a change of status identified by van Gennep. What we are wanting to suggest is that the process of change itself contains these 'moments', albeit of very varying lengths and intensity. This would be true not only for individual personal change, but for group and societal change as well.

Powers and dangers

Liminal people – that is, people regarded as being 'between' – are seen as at once powerful and dangerous. This has much to do with their threat to order: they highlight the fact that the lines of demarcation between one state and another, one thing and another, are not as clear and simple as we would like. The structural logic we talked about, underlying human behaviour and relations, also belongs to places and objects. The anthropologist Mary Douglas has written fascinatingly about dirt as 'matter out of place'. In her book *Purity and Danger*, she says: 'As we know it, dirt is essentially disorder. There is no such thing as absolute dirt: it exists in the eyes of the beholder ... Dirt offends against order. Eliminating it is not a negative movement, but a positive effort to organise the environment.' She goes on to give an example which we rather like:

I am personally rather tolerant of disorder. But I always remember how unrelaxed I felt in a particular bathroom which was kept spotlessly clean in so far as the removal of grime and grease was concerned. It had been installed in an old house in a space created by the simple expedient of setting a door at each end of a corridor between two staircases. The decor remained unchanged: the engraved portrait of Vinogradoff, the books, the gardening tools, the row of gumboots. It all made good sense as the scene of a back corridor, but as a bathroom – the impression destroyed repose. I, who rarely feel the need to impose an idea on external reality, at least began to understand the activities of more sensitive friends. In chasing dirt, in papering, decorating, tidying we are not governed by anxiety to escape disease, but are positively re-ordering our environment, making it conform to an idea.[4]

This is somewhat similar to the story of some friends who moved into a modern house on a rather smart housing estate in a small well-to-do town. They were keen vegetable growers and dug up their front lawn to plant runner beans and lettuces. Some surprise and complaint from neighbours might have been expected, but the upset their action caused pointed to a transgressing of some fundamental 'rule' about what belongs in the back garden and what belongs in the front.

The equation of dirt with disorder is relevant to our subject because it ties in with the way in which people who live between the structures of our society (those we often call 'marginal') are frequently described as 'dirty'. Although possible lack of access to a bathroom may mean that they are physically dirtier than their critics, it does not explain why this so-called dirtiness becomes the focus of so much negative attitude. We do not go on about the dirtiness of farmers, builders, or refuse collectors. Many people do, however, go on about the dirtiness of gypsies, the Convoy, or the women at Greenham Common.

Liminality is characterised by disorder; it is the place of chaos – at once creative and dangerous. Douglas explains the creative potential in disorder:

Granted that disorder spoils pattern; it also provides the materials of pattern. Order implies restriction; from all possible materials, a limited selection has been made and from all possible relations a limited set has been used. So disorder by implication is unlimited, no pattern has been realised in it, but its potential for patterning is indefinite. That is why, though we seek to create order, we do not simply condemn disorder. We recognise that it is destructive of existing patterns; also that it has potentiality. It symbolises both danger and power.[5]

This creative potential is reflected in the way in which holy people in some societies come to be recognised as having special sacred powers. 'Energy to command and special powers of healing come to those who can abandon rational control for a time.' So, for example, an Andaman Islander may leave his community and wander in the forest like a madman. When he returns to his senses and to his group, he has gained the occult power of healing. 'The man who comes back from those inaccessible regions brings with him a power not available to those who have stayed in the control of themselves and of society.'[6] Power resides in danger and in the indefinability of the transitional state, the threshold at which one is neither this nor that, neither one thing nor the other, and yet both.

Liminal not marginal

There is a good deal of talk in and around the churches about 'margins' and 'fringes'. This may be the somewhat derogatory description by those definitely on the inside ('They're both fringers') or the proud self-definition ('I like to be on the margins').

Much has been made of 'the margins': it is said to be the place of the prophet, the victim, the oppressed, the creative, the eccentric. 'Being on the margins' has become a vocation for some. It is certainly more often than not the place of the self-styled martyr.

The language of marginality *has*, however, provided a meaningful way of seeing and talking about the experience of not quite fitting into the church. Christians who describe themselves as being on the margins are those we have already mentioned: those who have rethought and left behind some of the church's traditional doctrines; those who experience exclusion or discrimination on grounds of their gender, race, class or sexual lifestyle; those who have a more general sense of not fitting, as well as some traditional religious communities.

Theologians and pastors have written much about marginality, in particular about the margins as the place of prophetic ministry. It also occurs frequently in the writings of those wishing to stress the prophetic role of monasticism. Thomas Merton, for example, described the monk as 'a marginal person ... who withdraws deliberately to the margin of society with a view to deepening fundamental human experience'.[7]

The language and image of marginality does, however, have a negative side to it. To define oneself as marginal is to define oneself in relation to someone else's centre; it is to accept another's definition of how things are. In that sense, it may be quite disempowering and in itself alienating. To have one's base and focus on the margins is to have a view of the present and the past; but what of the future?

We want to suggest that liminality offers an alternative and more creative language and image than that of marginality. The image of *threshold* has a more positive ring to it than that of *margin*. Threshold implies future. To be *between* here and there is to live in the faith that there is a future. To choose to be between here and there is to live in the faith that it will be a better future.

Liminality and change

As with the concept of marginality, following from Victor Turner's work in *The Ritual Process*, some writers have used the concept of liminality to analyse the nature and function of traditional religious communities. One such writer is

Richard Endress writing in the *American Benedictine Review* (Vol. 26, June 1975).

Endress focuses on the aspect of liminality which is to do with separation from normal society. He defines liminality 'as an ambiguous, sacred, social state in which a person or group of persons is separated for a time from the normal structure of society' (p. 142). He goes on to describe the different ways in which all human societies are structured and then offers two examples of liminal persons. The first is that of initiands in a rite of passage; the second is the example of persons who voluntarily separate themselves from society. This may be, for example, to prepare themselves for a major change in their lives. So he cites Jesus, the Buddha, Mohammed and others, who began their public ministries by first withdrawing. He also gives as examples those individuals or groups who withdraw from society to emphasise their opposition to its values, politics and so on. Such groups tend to proliferate at times of rapid social change and upheaval.

With this definition of liminality, which emphasises separation from society, it is not surprising that Endress views the monastic community as *the* example of a permanent liminal lifestyle, that is, a life of boundary-dwelling. (We shall comment on this further in the Epilogue, where we suggest a somewhat different emphasis.)

Liminal persons or groups have two important social functions. The first has to do with clarifying the basic structures of a society by highlighting the rearrangements of these structures that occur when change takes place. The second function has to do with the way in which liminal persons or groups bring about social change. Major social changes often begin when a small group sets itself apart and in opposition to the prevailing society; the wider society then slowly takes on the new values of the original protest group.

Endress sees monasticism as traditionally fulfilling both these functions for the church, again emphasising the apartness or separation of the monastic community. He sees the way in which they bring about change as the holding up of an ideal. In so doing he seems unfortunately (however unconsciously) to be using social anthropology to reassert the traditional view of the superiority of the monastic life. He writes:

> In seeking his own salvation the monk provides a model which the average Catholic may look up to and try to emulate, and the monastic community collectively provides a model of that ideal Christian community towards which the Church is presumably moving. All of this, I presume, is what is meant, at least partially, when monks speak about the prophetic role of their vocation.[8]

We would like at this point to introduce another, and perhaps more obvious example of a liminal community. The image of the women's camp at Greenham Common is a powerful and illuminating one when it comes to reflecting on the nature of boundary.

A military base guarding weapons of mass destruction. High security, guards, guns, blinding lights, razor wire. An ordinary Berkshire road, grey, winding, narrow in places. Houses: small, medium, large; bricks, curtains, warm lights, family homes. The razor wire and the road each provides a boundary not always easy to cross: they define the base and 'normal society'. Between them a verge: grass, bushes, mud, plastic sheeting, wood fires, women.

The women at Greenham were boundary-dwellers: they provided a visual, as well as a sociological, example of what it means to be between the structures of society; they were, in other words, liminal persons. The verge on which they camped represented the threshold between the military base and 'normal' civilian society. The women belonged to neither and yet to both. They were a constant threat to order because they regularly crossed boundaries and confused them. Their power (which was undeniable) stemmed essentially from their position, both physical and social. They dwelt in a no-place (here, literally a no man's land); they had no formal status. They attracted the strong ambivalent feelings directed at liminal persons: they were regarded with awe as special and were reviled as dirty and mad.

In this example the liminal persons are again instigators of change, not only because they hold an ideal, but because they challenge, cross and reshape boundaries. In a sense what the women at Greenham Common were about was the denial of separation or the refusal to allow the separation off from society and its human values of a military base where those values seemed suspended by the presence of weapons of mass destruction.

The women of the Greenham peace camp did separate themselves from 'normal society' for varying lengths of time, leaving families, jobs and homes for the time they spent in the camp. But their liminality has to do with their in-betweenness, and their living on a literal boundary, rather than their separateness.

Endress' description of monasticism as a liminal lifestyle highlights the feature of separation. The image of the women at Greenham Common reminds us that the liminal community is not only separated from normal social structures but is found *between* the structures of society and characteristically gathers and dwells on boundaries.

3

Wilderness

It has become fashionable to talk about 'wilderness spirituality'. Desert days and wilderness retreats begin to appear like a spiritual equivalent to the adventure holiday. The religious traveller is encouraged to venture forth and explore some of the more barren frontiers of faith. Rather like the package safari, there are all kinds of safety precautions and the traveller will return home at the end. It will have been an exciting experience, an interesting journey, one that can be shared with friends, back home, and remembered in photographs and souvenirs.

Holidays are good and sharing memories of them is good. But they are very different from other forms of travel adventure. Take the Bangladeshi refugee camped in the Jordanian desert, or the Bosnian stranded on the Austrian border, or the Cuban clinging precariously to a raft, or the political activist from . . . it could be anywhere, forced into exile. There is always hope of a return home some day, but that time away will not be measured in blocks of seven or fourteen nights at half-board. It is obscene to compare that kind of experience in a foreign land with a package holiday.

We suggest that there is a kind of parallel with the concept of wilderness spirituality. Retreats of a day or week into the 'wilderness' or 'desert' are good and memories of them are good, but they too are very different from some other forms of wilderness journey. In short, we have tamed and packaged the wilderness, thereby reducing its power – for good and evil – and denying the very real sense of 'homelessness' experienced by many Christians.

It is never very wise to take an analogy too far, but with the travel analogy the significance of 'home' is important. For refugees and exiles one of the agonising considerations is that, having been forced to leave their homes, they do not know when, or if, they will see them again. Home, of course, includes shelter, family, friends, culture, source of livelihood, and so on. The loss of many or most of these things holds true whether or not the exile or refugee is forced to face starvation and disease in a camp or live in relative physical comfort.

For the holidaymaker, on the other hand, the period of time away from home is nearly always fixed. Moreover, the degree of strangeness can to some extent be chosen; in a large Spanish resort it should not be too difficult to find bacon and eggs for breakfast and a group of English tourists to share them with. Even if you choose to go hiking in the Himalayas there is still the knowledge that back home in five or six weeks' time things will be much the same as when you left. In fact, when you go on holiday you don't really leave home at all, you are just away from it for a while.

We have lots of homes. Physical shelter and space to live is basic: to be homeless in this sense is intolerably stressful for most people and we have only to look at what happens to people on the street or to families in bed and breakfast accommodation to see this. We also talk of being 'at home' or 'feeling at home' in other ways and places: 'I feel at home in the Pentecostal Church'; 'I have found a home with this company'. Being at home or feeling at home says something about how we feel with certain people or in certain places: there is a sense of identification and affirmation, of something just 'fitting'. We are given a sense of security and a confirmation of who we are, as well as a kind of framework in which to be ourselves and to express ourselves. All these things are vital to us, literally life-giving. Without any sense of home at all it is hard to see how a person could survive.

What has all this to do with the wilderness and wilderness spirituality? Essentially, being in the wilderness for most people is about being in a place that is not home and that is not felt to be home. It may have to be a temporary 'home' but it does not contain those characteristics regarded as home: it is by its nature a place of journeying, not one of arrival.

Why then has it become a popular image? The argument of this book is that the concept of wilderness gives meaning to our experience of change, whether that change be in our personal lives as we face redundancy or a life-threatening illness, or whether it be concerned with the social dimensions of our religious attitudes and beliefs. If we are forced out of a job we enter the wilderness of financial insecurity and the haunting question of 'Who am I?' now that there is no job to be defined by. If biblical study, literary criticism, the Bishop of Durham, boredom, feminist analysis, or a new neighbourhood has made it impossibly painful to continue going to church, how do I express my religious faith? Both changes involve losing a home, a place that gives us a framework, or container, where we can be who we are and express who we are, in these instances through work and corporate worship. Change, even when it is desired, always involves loss. We have reflected so far on the personal and social dimensions of change; in this chapter we want to look at how Christian writers have perceived and written about the wilderness over the last three decades.

March 1965 saw the publication of Harry Williams' *The True Wilderness*,[1] a book which made an enormous impact on many Christians, both at the time of its publication and in the years following. Those who read it frequently reacted to its pages with great sighs of relief. Here was a spiritual writer, a priest and distinguished theologian, saying that it was OK to be human – not just OK, but that being human, being ourselves, was the way to God. *The True Wilderness* was the first of many books on spirituality to make human experience the stuff from which we learn about, and move towards, God. Williams resolved that:

> I would not preach about any aspect of Christian belief unless it had become part of my own life-blood. For I realized that the Christian truth I tried to proclaim would speak to those who listened only to the degree to which it was an expression of my own identity. (p. 8)

This was not so much a cool choice as the result of discovering that 'Unless what I proposed to say came from the depths of my own experience, I was struck dumb'.

Williams thus exhorts us to look for God in what we are and suggests that the experience is perhaps a 'theology of the self '. Thus began a decade or more of the psychologised gospel.

In *The True Wilderness*, Harry Williams focuses again and again on the themes of death and resurrection. If we acknowledge and allow death in our experience, we shall know growth and resurrection. It is a spirituality of personal struggle: the agony of the existentialist is never very far away. Williams writes:

> Human life is very largely a wilderness, a dry land where no water is. Riches are the artificial grass and plastic flowers with which we try to cover up the stony ground and persuade ourselves that we live in a watered garden. Death is the realistic acceptance of our wilderness for what it is, a refusal to cover it up with simulated appearances of life. Once we thus accept our wilderness and no longer try to hide it from ourselves, there follows the miracle of resurrection. (p. 12)

The wilderness for Williams is inside us, not outside, 'lurking somewhere as part of our experience . . . Our wilderness is an inner isolation. It's an absence of contact.' (p. 29) This might be a lack of contact with other people, or it might be an isolation from things formerly enjoyed that no longer give pleasure. This is not something we should deny or run away from, because such isolation is a necessary part or stage of being human.

Williams then relates this experience to the story of Jesus in the wilderness. The Spirit who drives Jesus there is the same Spirit who brought him the conviction of being called to do great things. The Spirit is none other than 'ourselves in the depths of what we are'. The story of Jesus in the wilderness is a confirmation that the wilderness is of God and that to feel isolated is part of our training in God's service. Our task is to recognise the wilderness for what it is, resist the temptation to denial or despair and accept the wilderness as ours.

In this particular sermon on the wilderness, and throughout the book, Williams speaks as one individual to other individuals. He is talking about personal spiritual journeys and each person's own human experience. We may share the experience, but my wilderness is my own inner wilderness, not one that we roam about in together. It is, as Williams states early on, inside us, not outside.

Less clear is the wilderness, or desert, of Carlo Carretto, a Little Brother of Jesus, who has written a number of popular books on spirituality including *Letters from the Desert, In Search of the Beyond,* and *The God who Comes.*[2]

Carretto writes not so much of 'wilderness', but of 'desert'.[3] The desert is the place of encounter with God. For Carretto, follower of Charles de Foucault, it was quite literally a desert – the Sahara. The desert experience is once again characterised by aloneness – not the agonising isolation of Williams' wilderness, but the 'joy of solitude' and silence: 'To learn to live these silences, the novice-master lets us go away for a few days "desert".'[4]

Carretto urges all Christians to find their own desert, for it is an essential component of the spiritual life.

When one speaks of the soul's desert, and says that the desert must be present in your life, you must not think only of the Sahara or the desert of Judaea, or into the High Valley of the Nile.

Certainly it is not everyone who can have the advantage of being able to carry out in practice this detachment from daily life ... And if you cannot go into the desert, you must nevertheless 'make some desert' in your life. Every now and then leaving men [sic] and looking for solitude to restore, in prolonged silence and prayer, the stuff of your soul. This is the meaning of 'desert' in your spiritual life.[5]

So desert experience, for Carretto, is also about detachment, letting go of the things of daily life in order to meet God in a more intense way. We are not encouraged to do this as an end in itself but rather so that we can meet God more fully in the same daily life we are encouraged to take a break from: '(But) the desert is not the final stopping place. It is a stage on the journey. Because ... our vocation is contemplation in the streets.' This may explain why the Foreword to Letters from the Desert was written by Carretto's friend, the great political activist and educationist, Ivan Illich. Although Carretto writes much about the individual soul, the desert is also the place where the perception of injustice and political sensibilities are sharpened.

However, it is in the writings of liberation theologians, from Latin America and elsewhere, that we see a political interpretation of the wilderness and wilderness imagery. For the story of the Exodus of the Israelites from Egypt becomes paradigmatic of all liberations from oppression: for the poor, for black people, for women, for homosexuals. 'The Exodus is the long march towards the promised land in which Israel can establish a society free from misery and alienation.'[6]

Here the journey in the wilderness is not an individual one, but the journey of a community, an oppressed people seeking to build a just and free society. 'The liberation of the Exodus was a mass movement. It entailed a whole people. The journey to the promised land did not take place by individuals acting in private.'[7]

This interpretation of the wilderness and the Exodus belongs not only to theologians of the Third World, but is also seen in the writings and liturgies of oppressed groups in our own society. When, for example, the Lesbian and Gay Christian movement was forced to move from its office in a London church, having been taken to an ecclesiastical court by the area dean, they marked their departure with a 'Service of Passover and Exodus' (10th September 1988).[8]

When women in the Southwark diocese wished to demonstrate their exclusion from priestly ministry in the Church of England, they held a Wilderness Liturgy outside Southwark Cathedral during the annual Petertide ordinations. That service is printed in full in an appendix and we shall talk about it in more detail in Chapter 6. However, let us note now the identification with the Exodus community, the corporate nature of the liturgy, and the link with creation through the imagery of the birth process in the reading from Isaiah 66. The wilderness becomes the time and place for the preparation of birth – the time and place of labour pains (an echo of Harry Williams' wilderness as that which necessarily precedes the experience of resurrection). It is once again the in-between – here, between conception and birth.

Over the last three decades, then, the wilderness has been used as an image of some aspect of the Christian spiritual journey. In the next two chapters there will be some further thoughts on biblical and later Christian experience of wilderness and desert, but for now we want to set out some of the characteristics and common threads of the wilderness image already mentioned.

First, a sense of aloneness. The person describing herself as being in the wilderness is saying something about being on her own at this stage of her journey. This may be the agonising sense of isolation and grief described by Williams, or it may be the joy of solitude and refreshment described by Carlo Carretto. Or, thirdly, it may be the sense of corporate separateness and exclusion experienced by whole groups –

for example, women or homosexual people in relation to the institutional churches. In each case the individual or the group experience themselves as in some sense away from 'home'; they find themselves not at home with themselves, not at home with their community, not at home with fellow-believers in the church.

The wilderness is also perceived as the place of encounter with God, even though it might not feel like that to those currently there. It is a place 'approved of' by God, where God is present, not absent. Indeed, it is a place into which God calls or drives people.

Finally, the wilderness has a temporary quality about it. It is the place entered before resurrection; it is the place of withdrawal between one episode of daily life and another; it is the place of journey and sojourn on the way to a more just and free society in which none is marginalised or oppressed. In essence, the wilderness is the place of in-between – the time of having left but not yet arrived. It is the state between what has been and what is yet to be. It represents an extended threshold of change.

Far from being concerned solely with some rather mystical and mystifying experience of the individual soul (whatever that is), the experience of wilderness has a broad social context, as a look around our world demonstrates. Most poignant, perhaps, were the revolutions in Eastern Europe which took place around Christmas 1989, the Gulf crisis around Christmas a year later, and the current civil war in what was Yugoslavia. The countries of Eastern Europe where communist rule was overthrown are still very much in an in-between state. The old order has gone, but the new is not yet in place. In the Gulf the border between Iraq and Kuwait has been destroyed and any new acceptable relationship has yet to be established. Such times are times to hold our breath. For the in-between is filled with chaos and the threat of disintegration, as well as the potential for new life. It is literally the old *order* which is destroyed.

The image of wilderness in recent spiritual writing relates to social experience as well as individual experience. The nature of our world means that we must find a way of making sense of the ambiguities of change and work out how, if at all, our religion can help us make the most creative use of that change. We believe that an image of the wilderness as the place of in-between offers us much in this area.

4

Revisiting the Bible

In this dark time of light ceasing between two days, Jacob awakens to the effectiveness of God's blessing. The hour of God's visitation sounds its intimate address at a mid-time, a dead stop, when Jacob belongs to no one, when he has left one home and not reached the other, when he has departed one place and not reached the other. The place where he can go no further because the sun has set, not because of his will but because of the earth's rhythm, this is the place he discovers to be 'the gate of heaven'.[1]

The image of the wilderness as the place of in-between has its origins, at least for Christians, in the Hebrew and Christian Testaments of the Bible.[2] To open the Bible, however, leads to a meeting and an exchange between human experience reflected in its pages and the reader's own experience.

Having looked at some everyday experiences of change and offered a model for understanding the process of change, in particular its pivotal phase, we wanted to revisit both the Bible and some aspects of Christian tradition wearing, as it were, liminally adjusted spectacles. So, the next two chapters depend on and reflect Jennifer's personal story within her own faith community. We invite you at the same time to look at your own encounter with the Bible and its images, and so reflect on your own experience of making transitions with or (apparently) without God.

Meanwhile, Jennifer sets out on her own revisiting.

The Hebrew Testament stories were a part of my childhood and of my growing up, but the first time I remember being jolted into a sense of active involvement with them was in the late 1950s, when a priest of the Community of the Resurrection led my local congregation one Holy Week out of Egypt, through the Red Sea and across the desert to within sight of the Promised Land. The great transit or passover of Jesus from life through death to resurrection was presented and liturgically re-presented in the language of his own forebears and in terms of one of the key moments of change in their history. We were given to understand that we too were taking part in a march of liberation, a march which led us by way of the cross to the Easter garden. In many a later Holy Week this journey was far more tense and grindingly awful, the gap more nearly uncrossable – for a whole variety of reasons – but there it was that I caught the message that we, as the people of God, were on the move, *out of* slavery, *across* terrain so dark and difficult that we could not make it on our own (though we were united as at no other time by the sense of the grandeur of the action we were part of) and (however weak, fearful and exhausted) *into* the land of promise. In an earlier year I had heard the *Exsultet* sung on Easter Eve by a competent Cambridge musician; in the parish the churchwarden's sweet, true tenor collected us all up more unpretentiously; in later years, as a member of a religious community I was sometimes asked to sing the *Exsultet* myself, so that even if the chaplain could not sing, 'the ransomed of the Lord' should 'come with singing to Sion'. Never more truly have I known 'the moment of real change, the pivotal moment that has no movement of itself, but permits movement to take place'.

Later I might question how far Christians could make use of this Hebrew story and imagery as totally our own; might question what the price of Hebrew liberation was (and is) for the other inhabitants of the Promised Land; might question the ease with which the elaborate and powerful liturgy of the Paschal Feast could co-exist with a fairly unawakened, self-contented liberalism, corporately and individually introverted and self-absorbed. (Yes, there was Christian CND, and there were Christian pacifist organisations, and Christian Action was beginning its fight against apartheid in South Africa; but liberation theology had not yet emerged, nor Christian feminism, nor the massive dislocations of the eighties.) All the same, in that Holy Week I found in a changing world my place in a community itself 'on the move'.

In the thirty-five years since, there have been many other awakenings, dislodging the solid defences of a fortress-style Christianity and with them the unstudied expectations of a society that has been changing, it seems, in spite of itself. When I first came across Charles Williams' aphorism 'Nothing is certain: everything is safe', another door opened to freedom, though my first reaction was to say, 'But that's exactly the opposite of what I've always thought!'

For many, Christians as well as others, the disintegrative developments in church as in society have been more than they can bear. The place-between is indeed dark, chaotic, full of dangerous elements and experiences. The fundamentalist revival is one way of trying to cope with these. Those who embody such elements and experiences are declared to be marginal, fringe-people (and they often accept the definition). Others more or less quietly despair. What I find given is that the safe God is not a fortress but a companion, protean (many-featured and elusive), often unrecognised and unrecognisable, not tame, a 'someone' who is not contained even by the loftiest available notions of personal relationship.

So now I am about to look at some themes and events of the Hebrew and Christian Testaments with my head full of the ideas that cluster round the image of wilderness: ideas of change, of transition, of leaving and loss, of movement towards a new place, of danger and temptation, new opportunity, even divine encounter. A question immediately arises: Is the Bible part of the half-forgotten, mourned for, despised, boring, uncomplicated world of that time when we were (more or less) contented, blind-eyed like new-born kittens that scramble for milk from a resigned parent till the moment comes when, eyes opening, they begin to move away? If this were the case, there would certainly be no point in this chapter. However, Christians in the wilderness will still, many of us, be looking to all the sources that formerly sustained us to see where we may again find meaning, and new meaning at that: where we may engage with the experience of our forebears and predecessors on this religious trail, and shape, sharpen and direct (in some degree) our own experience. And this is a range of activity that absorbs all who have ever, for whatever reasons, been driven by some form of divine discontent.

All the same, readers of the Bible may make many strange assumptions, which, like old clothes, need to be shaken out, reassessed, and made over for the present task. First among these is the notion that many of us (apart from the academically trained) tend to hold, that one can begin from the Bible, as though it were a static starting-point, as though it contains all interpretations of itself that ever were or shall be, as though we could, for the asking, tap its 'view' of things without ourselves being involved in the content of what we discover, or even in the process of discovery. To give an example of what I mean: an anxious woman (say) decides to open the Bible at random (but with prayer) to find a 'word' from God for her own situation. She opens at a page in Mark's Gospel and sees the words: 'She has done what she could.' At once she feels relief and gratitude, a freeing of the spirit, a vindication. The religious value of such an exercise may be not inconsiderable, but it is clearly at least as dependent on the state of mind and heart of the reader as on the Bible passage 'in itself'.

So we cannot look at the Bible to see 'what is there', as we might go to the larder to see what the jam supply is like. Whether we engage with the biblical texts critically or contemplatively (and all good scholars have something of the contemplative, just as all real contemplatives have a strong element of the sceptic in their make-up) we are involved in a two-way process, in which the text and the reader are, in terms of understanding, equally important.

In a very real sense, too, our engagement with the image of wilderness in the Bible comes at the end, not at the beginning, of our exploration: we are the product of centuries of study and reflection and response by our forebears. We are not fresh, untouched by any of the past: quite the opposite, of course, and there is nothing wrong with that. Nevertheless, it makes some sense to connect the biblical generations (a thousand years or more of them) with our own before looking for a few vantage points to survey the years between. Anyone who attempts this for themselves would do well to reckon up their own range of experience of the Bible. As is clear from the opening of this chapter, what is offered here is reflection arising from a contemporary experience of the Bible, not least in the context of liturgical worship in the cycle of the Christian year. There can also be added the reading of modern commentaries (with varying degrees of respect) and older or ancient commentaries (with a mixture of bewilderment and delight), and the experience of Ignatian and other retreats, where the chief problems are not in the end those posed by biblical criticism but those posed by the tendency towards privatising the scriptures. What follows will represent a multi-focal engaging with the scriptures as a member of the human race, the Christian Church, the Anglican Communion, the community of women in and around the churches. The reader is invited here to take stock of his or her own range of experience of the Bible: it can be surprising to discover how rich and varied and one's own this experience is.

The Hebrew and Christian Testaments each contain one outstanding wilderness event: the post-Exodus forty years of wandering in the wilderness by the Israelite tribes before their entry into the 'promised land', and the forty-day sojourn by Jesus in the wilderness after his baptism and before the start of his public ministry. In both instances the wilderness is the place and time between, a time and place of transition: something has ended, something else not yet begun. The between-time may have a certain measured containment, but the between space is distinguishable by its no-where-ness: it is a real 'no man's land', away from ordinary everyday settled existence and the places appropriate to that. The entry into the wilderness is sparked off by a moment or moments of supreme significance: before the Exodus there were signs and wonders, but preceding them all was the revelation at the Burning Bush. Israel is God's firstborn son (Exodus 4:22). Jesus' baptism is presented as one of the moments of recognition of his nature and destiny; immediately afterwards the Spirit drives him into the wilderness, the place deeply embedded in the consciousness of his people as the place of naked encounter with both good and evil; a place of danger, and of enormous opportunity, without ordinary means of sustenance, or human company; a necessary 'between-time', which cannot be shortened or shirked; a time of tempting, and of testing. In the Hebrew Testament the Israelites are tested by the Lord who has claimed them as his own people; in the narratives of the Synoptic Gospels, Jesus, the son in whom his father delights, is tempted by Satan. This post-Apocalyptic heightened dualism in the Judaism of Jesus' time has left its mark on generations of Christians, who perhaps more readily talk of temptation than of testing. But ambiguity and ambivalence are in both cases sharpened beyond what seem like ordinary powers of endurance: the Israelites fall, over and over again (Psalm 78); Jesus might seem almost smugly right every time, by contrast, but in fact what the evangelists mean to suggest (as Mark's account shows clearly, without detailing the 'temptations' at all) is that the stage is here set for the struggle that lies ahead.

The desert is a place/time of transition. Such place/times have characteristic features, visible on a grand scale in the story of the journey of the people of Israel through the wilderness. Something has been left behind: Egypt, at first a place of refuge in the days of Joseph and his brethren, had become a place of slavery. Israel had come out of Egypt, had been delivered from the wrath of Pharaoh through the strong right arm of Israel's God and the leadership of his servant Moses.

But the destination, the promised land, has not yet been reached: in fact it is many years' away, the years of wandering in the wilderness.

The wilderness: in spite of the fact that desert regions did include pasture land and settlements, the various words translated as 'desert' or 'wilderness' have deep underlying associations in Hebrew thought, which emerge all through the Hebrew and indeed Christian Testaments. The wilderness is the place where God did not exert God's life-giving activity; the abode of wild animals and unclean spirits: [in Babylon overthrown] 'wild animals will lie down there, and its houses will be full of howling creatures; there ostriches will live, and there goat-demons will dance. Hyenas will cry in its towers, and jackals in the pleasant palaces' (Isaiah 13:21-2); 'When an unclean spirit goes out of someone it wanders through waterless country looking for a place to rest' (Matthew 12:43). It is 'a land not sown' (Jeremiah 2:2), a place 'in which there is no man' (Job 38:26), 'a howling wilderness waste' (Deuteronomy 32:10).

So the wilderness is an unfamiliar, strange and dangerous place, into which people have been thrust as much as led by their own choosing, a place likely to give occasion for fear, disappointment, nostalgia for what has been left behind ('the fleshpots of Egypt'), and the temptation to despair and 'tempt the Lord'. Supplies may be found, but they are meagre, and the spirit droops at the prolonged hardness of the journey.

Nevertheless, the wilderness was a refuge for a fugitive people; and, much more, a sacred place: as the Hebrews came to see it, their God not only brought them into this in-between place, but went with them, was guiding them in the pillar of cloud by day and of fire by night, the same God who could 'turn a desert into pools of water, a parched land into springs of water' (Psalm 107:35), and provide manna in the wilderness. And over and above it all, the wilderness was the setting for the revelation on Mount Sinai, the divine– human encounter which issued in the giving of the Law and the establishing of Israel's self-identity as a royal and priestly people.

'The internally allusive character of the Hebrew texts . . . is more like the pervasive allusiveness of Eliot's *The Waste Land* or Joyce's *Ulysses* than, say, the occasional allusiveness of Wordsworth's *The Prelude*.'[3] Robert Alter's comment could stand as a text for what follows in this present chapter. One can point to certain other key moments in Hebrew history where 'the wilderness' has a leading role, above all for the exilic prophets, writing to encourage their people exiled in Babylon, looking for another Exodus, another deliverance. This time, says the prophet, 'the wilderness and the dry land shall be glad, the desert shall rejoice and blossom . . . waters shall break forth in the wilderness, and streams in the desert; the burning sand shall become a pool, and the thirsty ground springs of water; the haunt of jackals shall become a swamp, the grass shall become reeds and rushes' (Isaiah 35:1,7). This time, the way of the Lord will be pre- pared in the wilderness, a straight highway, with valleys lifted up and mountains and hills made low, the uneven ground made level and the rough places a plain (the vigour and beauty of the language in any of our translations all but disguises the strangeness, indeed, to our mind, the violence of the imagery: not a gospel text for the environmentalist); and across this highway the Lord's redeemed will return with joy and singing to Zion. For these people there will be a new covenant, a new law written on the heart. Once again, the desert journey is associated with an in-between time, however different the circumstances, both in fantasy and in reality.

The forty days that Jesus is said to have passed in the wilder- ness, driven there by the Spirit immediately after his baptism by John, were for him a time of transition, more appropriately compared with the forty days spent by Moses and by Elijah in solitary fasting than with the forty years of wandering after the Exodus from Egypt. It is a transition within a larger process of transition. Jesus left behind a more or less private, settled, even rather pre-conscious existence, and looked towards a much more public life and ministry. The testing by Satan is a sign of what is to come, envisaged in terms familiar to the Judaism of his day; and the God whose hand was upon him at his baptism was with him in this first real taste of wilderness life. 'He was with the wild beasts, and angels ministered to him.' At the very end of his life, another significant time of transition comes: between baptism and public ministry lies the time in the wilderness 'tempted by Satan'; between his death on the cross and Easter Day lies the all-important Holy Saturday, the 'descent into hell'.

But while I am still preoccupied with the ideas associated with the wilderness, I find quite fruitful, in the light of my own faith journey and that of the whole community of faith to which I belong in its diverse forms, the perception of Jesus' ministry as his 'way through the wilderness'.[4] This is not at all the same as seeing everything and everyone of significance in the Hebrew Testament as a type of Christ and of his experiences. On the other hand, it is not at all surprising if Jesus and later the evangelists found that the language of the Hebrew Testament best held the meaning of his life and ministry. Mauser's book is a study in Mark's Gospel, in which there are only a few references to the wilderness as such after the forty-day period following his baptism. But the mountain and the sea also carry many of the associations of the 'wilderness places', and although these sound like more or less static geographical features, they are settings for events that happen to a man and a people on the move, on a religious journey, steeped in the language and memories of their Hebrew ancestors. The transfiguration of Jesus is described in terms that gather up many of these allusions: the withdrawal, after a six-day pause, to a high mountain apart, where two of the great Hebrew men of the wilderness appear to converse with Jesus, where the disciples want to establish the traditional sign of God's presence with the people in the setting up of tents or booths, where the cloud indicates God's hidden presence and the voice from it comes as a new moment of revelation. Yet the revelation is not of a work completed but (as Luke's Gospel spells out) a looking towards the 'exodus' that Jesus was to accomplish. If the feeding of the crowds in the wilderness seems to echo the experiences of Israel fed by manna in the wilderness, the sense of a people on the move is made clear. If Jesus, the lonely Galilean (as Mauser calls him), understands the Baptist's repentance as the call to a life of persistence in the desert, does he show many signs of recognising the loss of what he has had to leave behind? Some might use this chance to say 'There! You see? The true hero does not have time for regrets!' Of course the gospel-writers present him as setting his face firmly towards the task ahead and, ultimately, towards Jerusalem. But there are incidents (his abrupt, not to say rude, treatment of his family) and sayings ('the Son of Man has nowhere to lay his head'; 'Leave the dead to bury the dead'; 'No one who puts a hand to the plough and looks back is fit for the kingdom of God') that seem to indicate a strong sense of having to count the cost, which is part of what registering loss is about.

Thus far I have cursorily revisited the two definitive 'wilderness' events of the Hebrew and Christian Testaments, without having tried to set up an unbreakable paradigm for the 'authentic' wilderness experience, to which every experience and event of our own lives has to be matched. The passage quoted as an epigraph to this chapter shows that the 'wilderness' experience can be found on a relatively small scale, quite tellingly, sharpening our perspective on the incident related and on events and times in our own lives which in some way resemble these ancient stories. For myself, if I look to wrestling Jacob with something like awe, I can approach the story of Hagar in Genesis 16 and 21 with greater ease, even though I know I am on difficult ground with her – she has been the occasion of feminist indignation at the treatment of women in the undoubtedly patriarchal religion of the Hebrew Testament.[5] At this moment I choose to read the story as I find it in the Bible: inconsistent with itself, because the two parts come from different sources, but still a moving and meaningful story, offering points of identification with experiences of other people at other times. In chapter 16 the story is hers, after verse 6, though Sarai is the 'mainline' character of Israel's history. Hagar *is* important: she is the mother of Ishmael, the son of Abraham: Ishmael is not only the son of Abraham but also the forebear of a great nation. Ill-treated by Sarai, the pregnant Hagar runs away into the desert, and there is met by 'the angel of the Lord'. She is the first biblical figure (Trible points out) 'to be visited by a divine messenger; the only one to name God; the first woman in Israel's memory to hear an annunciation and bear a child; the only woman to receive a divine promise of descendants'. The first episode ends with her return to servitude and to Sarai, but with all this divine encounter and promise. The second episode is her final expulsion with her child, again at the instigation of Sarai (now Sarah), though this time with the active assistance of Abraham, after the birth of Isaac. Once more she is alone in the desert, facing danger of death for herself and her child. Once more the angel of the Lord speaks to her to instruct and help her and to promise a great future for her son. This time the resolution of the crisis involves her finding in the desert her permanent home. The story is now really Ishmael's, and I am no doubt removing it from its context to find a satisfying and in some ways moving account of a twofold transition. But it is all there: the loss of place (and face), the desert as a place of danger and of divine encounter, the re-establishment in ways that build on the experience of being 'in between' places and families and (it might almost seem) the plans of God. If this is a crude 'tribal' story, there is remarkable respect accorded the one who inevitably comes off second-best.

Another very brief allusion, which tantalisingly suggests a whole wilderness transition, is a phrase in Paul's reference in Galatians 1:17 to his sojourn in 'Arabia', immediately after his conversion and first preaching. What was this about? Many years ago I enjoyed enormously reading Bishop Lightfoot's learned note on this verse,[6] in which he develops the hypothesis that Paul in fact withdrew into the desert of Sinai, following the footsteps of Moses and Elijah, as befitted a man who had to make an enormous adjustment in his religious faith and outlook. Of course one does not have to suppose that everything is stated in the New Testament material about Paul, or that there is only one right way to interpret it. But it does make sense to suppose that, after an extraordinary change of heart, time apart was needed to adjust to the changed perspective. Paul was well aware of what he had lost – he goes on about it quite forcefully, in passages like that in the letter to the Philippians (3:4–6) – and it would be doing him and his new faith less than justice to suppose that he did not have to withdraw for a time to come to terms with what he had to let go as well as what he had gained.

This chapter must end, however, with my own adjustment to a way of looking at the shared worship of the community of faith, a way which in part I found for myself and in part recognised in the post-Vatican II liturgical renewal by the monastic orders, especially the Benedictine Order, which came up with something like a new theology of the divine office.[7] They saw the worshipping community, on every occasion that it met to celebrate the divine office, as placing itself with Christ to make with him, in the power of the Spirit, the 'passover' to God his Father that only he could carry through. Put thus briefly and bluntly it may sound a rather simplistic attitude, but it represented for me, and for many others, a liberation from a rather stifling sense of never-ending obligation 'to offer praise to the Holy Trinity'. It was like being delivered from a guilt-inducing treadmill on to a moving vehicle – not always a chariot of fire, but at least always a kind of pilgrim train, on which all sorts of experiences of loss, change, insight and discovery, pain and desire, could be carried, and one's sights set on a goal worth waiting and striving for.

The silence of Holy Saturday (Easter Eve), the in-between day, is enormously significant.

What is happening? Today there is a great silence over the earth, a great silence, and stillness, a great silence because the king sleeps; the earth was in terror and was still because God slept in the flesh and raised up those who were sleeping from the ages.[8]

Now I saw where he who was like the Son of Man opened the prison-house and led out his own, whom he had redeemed; and they followed him singing, Hosanna to the King of Israel! This is our God; we have waited for him; we will be glad and rejoice in his salvation. Then in his light they followed where he went before, and I followed after; the eyes of the blind were opened, and they saw him, and he led them out.[9]

5

Centuries of Wilderness: 'They seek a better country'

From the Christian Testament, via the desert fathers and mothers, to Harry Williams, Carlo Carretto and Gustavo Gutierrez, the wilderness or desert has been an enduring image of the Christian way. The experience of human life as itself transient and as a time of transitions full of 'changes and chances' has been nourished and supported by such teaching.

Christian tradition is long and contains numerous perspectives. In choosing what in Christian tradition to revisit in this chapter, monasticism and the spirituality of the desert would have provided an obvious focus (briefly touched on in what follows). But that perspective is somewhat remote for most of us. One of the assumptions of this book is that the experience of change is something we *all* have to grapple with and that whilst we may live in an age of particularly rapid change, men and women throughout history have had to come to terms with change in their lives. In revisiting Christian tradition and teaching, the questions that seemed most interesting were those to do with what happened to ordinary (lay) people's perceptions of life's changes. How have these been reported or presented? What wisdom has been gained from such experience?

When Jennifer reflected on this she realised that among the writers whose influence was important to her as she grew up in the 1940s and 1950s were four lay Anglicans: Evelyn Underhill, Charles Williams, Dorothy L. Sayers and C. S. Lewis. In some cases it was easy enough to see how their experience of change affected their attitudes and their writing; in others, the writing itself explores moments of crisis and change, in various different contexts, not always explicitly religious. This led further to the memory of creative writers not necessarily Christian but certainly people of notable spiritual quality, who threw further light on the processes of change.

Once again Jennifer sets out on a personal revisiting wearing her liminally adjusted spectacles, this time re-viewing ways in which Christians of earlier times have struggled with and found meaning in their experience of change.

As long as the Parousia, the Second Coming of Christ, was perceived as imminent, the wilderness of the waiting time was what mattered, the laying aside of lesser cares, the watchfulness, the expectation. As this sense of imminence began to stretch out into an unknown future, the Christian community began to be a recognised stratum of society and eventually a respectable part, at length *the* respectable, official religious dimension of its society. When this moment came, some Christians were already disappearing 'outside the gate', drawn to unpopulated areas to carry on the inner warfare of the spirit. They were acutely aware of the need to be ready. They saw all this life as a time of passage, and the Christian's task as to be always ready for the return of the householder 'at an hour you do not know'. The desert fathers and mothers did not necessarily live in remote places – they needed a local market for their simple handcrafts or produce, and sometimes, like Daniel the Stylite on his pillar near the Bosphorus, they were available for consultation by secular rulers and princes. Over the centuries memorable insights were gained into the workings of the human spirit and psyche. The Holy Mountain of Athos in the East and Benedictine monasticism in the West, along with the later canons regular, and others, became the repositories and schools of a spiritual wisdom that seized on the imagery of wilderness in the Bible and made it an important cornerstone of their experience and teaching on 'life apart'. On the whole we have the stories and the teachings of those who left marriages (if they married at all), or lived 'chastely' within marriage, or felt themselves to be second-rate if they did not aspire to a state higher than matrimony in this life. As things are, or have been, even with the increased literacy (and individualism) of the later Middle Ages and the Reformation and Counter-Reformation, the great teachers are mostly celibates living an other than ordinary life as far as management of choices and of possessions is concerned. The riches of their discoveries and the inspiration of their lives have nourished the ground of Christian discipline from below and watered it from above, but for teacher and pupil the world remained 'this weary wilderness' from birth to death, a vale of tears if also of soul-making.

Where monasticism dies out the teachers are still the clerics, even though the clerics may now be married. Bursts of lay activity (for example, the beginnings of the Society of Friends) either begin or end in antagonism to more institutionalised bodies like the national church. Their teaching is often self-contained and by and large self-containing, wilderness teaching, indeed, in that it deliberately stands apart from the mainstream and often enough looks forward with renewed fervour to the Lord's coming as its own vindication. But even these lay groups and others are only known to us because of their being literate, even when their writings were suppressed by opponents. Without decrying the enormously rich and varied treasury of centuries of Christian insight into the ways of the Spirit in the lives of human beings, we are still left with the fact that the teachers have mostly been monks, nuns or clerics, their lives set apart from much of the common stuff of human existence. Andrew Louth's recent interesting book, *The Wilderness of God*,[1] provides a fine example: he ends with a study of the value T. S. Eliot placed on the desert tradition and how it influenced his poetic vision. But the book itself is about the tradition that began when the earliest Christians' sense of being 'aliens and foreigners' in their world was succeeded by a period when some came to feel that it was all too easy to become comfortably at home in the society of the Christian Empire, and began to move away in ones and twos and larger numbers into the less populated areas outside the cities and villages.

What have we to learn from those who over the centuries have stayed at home, where most of us find ourselves? To be sure, we may know the 'desert in the city' (as those earlier Christians sought to establish the city in the desert) – the city as a place of spiritual loneliness and struggle. To be sure, we can only expect to tap the wisdom of those who were able to write, or speak to those who wrote down their message. One can't help smiling at Augustine's North African congregation crying out in dismay (as he himself reports) as he pointed out to them that the forgiveness of their sins depended entirely on their readiness to forgive those who offended against them; it is a shock to realise that women in Bede's day were expected to absent themselves from Holy Communion during their periods. Such people do not speak for themselves, and we can only guess how they felt and believed. The elaborate provision, made by those who could afford it, for masses to be said for their souls after their death (even the moderately prosperous William and Margaret Paston in the fifteenth century each provided for seven years of daily masses) gave a sense of continuity with past generations and a reaching ahead to those who would survive their death.

In an age like our own when far fewer Christians are called to a celibate life, let alone a lifelong monastic or religious profession, it is widely recognised that lay people have a task to take up, a wisdom to discover and to voice. This wisdom is not something entirely different from that accumulated over the Christian centuries, but it does contain a new ingredient that can come only from the circumstances and experiences of lay people. They are professed Christians only but decisively by their baptism or conversion and by their determination to be disciples of Jesus, seeking God's reign

and righteousness in purity of heart just as truly as did John
Cassian and those whose teaching he recorded in the fourth
century.

There was a hymn sung occasionally in the parish church of
my New Zealand youth, perhaps even then appreciated more
by those nearer the end of their lives than the beginning. It
included the lines:

> Here in the body pent
> Absent from Him I roam
> And nightly pitch my moving tent
> A day's march nearer home.[2]

We might exclaim: Did the desert journey have to include
such strong dualism (even with Pauline overtones)? Other
favourites were 'O happy band of pilgrims', 'Through the
night of doubt and sorrow', 'Brief life is here our portion',
'Jerusalem the Golden': the whole course of life as a way
through the desert to the promised land of heaven is here
clear enough. A veering away from the rather melancholy
tone of such hymns can produce words and tunes more
sentimental or more jaunty, but hardly more solidly robust.

Perhaps the commonest attitude to 'changes and chances'
is to claim the companionship ('Abide with me') of the Lord
('thou who changest not') on the journey. This no doubt
can be a robust attitude, but it can also become something
like a divine insurance policy, to be saved for a rainy day.
'Lead, kindly light', especially sung to the tune 'Sandor',
can sound quite mawkish. When one recalls that 'Abide
with me' is based on the Emmaus story, one cannot help
wondering what has happened to the spirit of those two who
rose up straight away, eventide or not, and hurried back to
Jerusalem to tell of their encounter with Jesus 'on the way'.

In other words, the need is for lay Christians to look for
the presence and the challenge that the wilderness represents
in all those ordinary and extraordinary, small- and large-
scale changes and chances of everyday living. How does the

religious faith of lay Christians affect the way they meet and traverse the great gaps or 'desert' moments that affect every human life in some way or another? Some such gaps, as we have seen earlier in this book, are truly 'vales of misery', obvious times of loss and change: the death of loved ones and the consequent bereavement, or separation through estrangement and divorce; the terrors and anxieties of times of war, even for those who have not experienced displacement as refugees or the worse horrors of 'ethnic cleansing' or political oppression in various forms. These 'gaps', as has often enough been pointed out by attentive observers of the present world scene, seem to multiply and even overlap, so that all of us are affected to some extent by the spectacle and the experience of a world in the grip of terrible destructive forces, struggling against disintegration in every imaginable way. We have also, however, seen some passages 'from death to life' – at least as experienced by a significant number of those affected – for instance, in Eastern Europe and in South Africa. And there are clearly vast numbers among us who make our personal or communal transitions, not without struggle, but with courage, patience, energy and dogged effort. If we can learn to see the processes of change in our own lives and in those of the smaller and larger communities of which we are part in terms that do not barricade against fear by means of sentimentality, nor martyrise ourselves on the margins of church or society, then we shall gain in courage and in discernment and in energy.

Since it is rather unfair to establish a line of argument on the basis of the hymns people may or may not sing, I turn to look again at the four lay Anglicans mentioned at the start of this chapter. Perhaps it is worth observing that all but Evelyn Underhill (and possibly she too) were drawn to writing not least because they needed to supplement the income of their household. What were the notable transitions of their lives? How did they weather their storms? Where is the fruit of their own or others' teaching as Christians to be seen? (I might have included T. S. Eliot, but ahead of him comes Edwin Muir, a Christian even if not a churchy one –

more of him later.) In ways more or less obvious, their
writings, whether directly religious and theological or not,
were clearly affected by moments and periods of sharply felt
change in their lives. Also, especially as writers of religious
fiction, they inevitably and often strikingly describe some of
life's gaps.

Evelyn Underhill

In 1907, after a long period of very gradual development,
she 'was "converted", quite suddenly, once and for all, by
an overpowering vision which ... convinced me that the
Catholic religion was true'.[3] For her at that time, this experience amounted to a summons to join the Roman Catholic
Church. But she was preparing for her marriage, which also
took place in 1907 (July), and for her fiancé this step of
hers was just about unthinkable. These two people, whose
families had been friends since their childhood, had now, in
their thirties, after years of close and easy friendship and
comradeship, come to the point of embarking on marriage
together. It seems that the area of religious faith was not
part of the bond of their intimacy, and this has puzzled some
of Evelyn Underhill's admirers, who have sometimes been
inclined to write off Hubert Stuart Moore as the rather
dull background against which Evelyn's intellectually and
spiritually outstanding capacities developed. But others who
remembered them have thought differently, and her marriage may well have been the needed personal container or
shelter, a relationship of trust and friendship that gave her
human security in her long spiritual search, which had begun
much earlier, and which outlasted the years of spiritual chaos
and confusion referred to here. Her husband's misgivings
about the Roman Catholic Church held her back, and in
the same year the encyclical *Pascendi gregis* appeared to
demand 'a surrender of her intellectual honour' which she
could not make. Charles Williams, admittedly in his own
quite distinctive style, sums up her situation thus: 'She dis-
sented, and was inflexibly called, she assented, and was

inflexibly refused.' 'She was between two impossibilities.'[4] In this same year she began work on *Mysticism*, subtitled *A study in the nature and development of man's spiritual consciousness*. She began, in Williams' words, to 'live with that impossibility'. Interestingly enough, the beginning of her work on mysticism seems to have coincided with the ending of her connection with the occultist Order of the Golden Dawn. She worshipped, and prayed, and read, and studied, and wrote, and gave modestly from what she was learning to people who began to consult her. Her already existing habits of thoroughness in whatever pursuits she undertook stood her in good stead. Her passage was made easier by her acquaintance with some of the Roman Catholic Modernists, in particular Baron von Hügel, under whose guidance she finally committed herself to incarnational Christianity and the Anglican Church. When she heard from the Franciscan Sorella Maria her 'word', 'in tormento e travaglia servire i fratelli',[5] she could recognise a counterpart to her own experience and practice. As a mature spiritual writer and guide, her concern remained with the possibilities of ordinary life, and the nourishment it needs. Much of her personal story remains obscure to us, and her style of living far removed from the present-day world, but her passage through the constraints of 1907 is sufficiently visible to offer both a personal example and as it were a textbook instance of the dangers and possibilities of crises of change.

It seems that her predilection for the homeliness of a recognised, truly creaturely relationship to God arose from the same capacities that enabled her to traverse the difficult 'borderland' years when her spiritual search was intense and without human resting place. In one of her last collections of retreat addresses, there is an illustration worth quoting at length, full of her characteristic insight:

The journey of the soul through life is strangely like the progress of the child Alice through Looking-glass Land. For both the plot has an active, visible and obvious side, and a quiet, deeply-hidden mysterious side. Alice, that small representative of the spirit of man, finds herself wandering through a strange, unstable world of circumstance, and undergoing many bewildering experiences which seem, as the experiences of our life often do, chaotic and unmeaning. She travels through a country which is divided like a chessboard into light and dark patches. She has no map and little sense of direction; and she passes for no apparent reason, and in no apparent sequence, from square to square. The odd people whom she meets, and the odd things which happen, seem quite unconnected with the game. Everything is in a muddle; most disconcerting to those who expect to find the clue to life's meaning in the tangle of daily events.

But if we turn back to the first page of this bewildering story, we find there what Alice wanted but could never discover: a plan of the chessboard as the Player sees it, with each piece in its right position in relation to the whole. Then we see that everything which happened to Alice, however unmeaning, disconcerting or apparently hostile to her interests, was a real move in a real game. All these changes and chances, these pains and frustrations, were queer but deliberate devices for getting the child, who began as a pawn, to the eighth square, where she must end as a Queen. The help and direction she received from the creatures that she encountered, the imperceptible pressure of events never varied in intention. However great the obstacles, the apparent confusions and absurdities, the goal was always the eighth square. The best advice was often that which seemed most foolish; as when the Rose told Alice to walk away from the Red Queen if she wanted to meet her. The really important moves were not recognized till long after they were made. It is true that Alice went through one of the earlier squares by train; but she was actually passing through another, almost at the end of her journey, when she thought herself hopelessly lost in the dark forest with nothing to help her but the muddled statements of the White Knight. Once she was called right off the path to befriend the silly and untidy old White Queen. Yet it was in running after the Queen's lost shawl, and jumping the little brook over which it had floated, that Alice made her next move, and reached the fifth square. . . . In spite of her bewilderment the child caught in the web of circumstance was never really lost; each baffling experience contributed something to the whole. The hand of the Player was hovering over the Pawn.[6]

C. S. Lewis

If marriage accompanied a time of crisis for Evelyn Underhill, of C. S. Lewis it could be said that it was a death, the death of his mother when he was not quite ten years old, that opened up for him an emotional chasm which he traversed, if at all, only in the last years of his life some fifty years later after the death of his wife. Much has been written about Lewis, and I am not competent to enter the fray. For how many young men of his generation was not the First World War an abyss of horror, ultimately death-bringing? If Mrs Moore, the mother of a dead acquaintance, came to fill the emotional gap left by his mother's death ten years earlier, who can be surprised? Perhaps only those who drink in every word of the Christian apologist that Lewis became, and who somehow blindly assume that everything about him must be marked by a robust, felicitous inerrancy like that conveyed to many readers by his style of writing. His description of his father in *Surprised by Joy* (1955) is confusing, as it is then hard to see how such a caricature of a man could, in the weeks after his death, have been such a help as his son claimed, in the same son's struggle against the necessity of succumbing to a form of orthodox Christian faith. This same C. S. Lewis could say after the unexpected death of a close friend some fifteen years later: 'No event has so corroborated my faith in the next world as Williams did simply by dying. When the idea of death and the idea of Williams thus met in my mind, it was the idea of death that was changed.'[7]

Lewis had just finished writing *The Great Divorce*,[8] an

account in fantasy form of hell and heaven, the gap between (so huge and yet as small as that between two blades of grass), and the sort of habitual attitudes that can make hell into purgatory or purgatory into hell. It is a cultured, cultivated book, easy to read even now when the confidence of its style grates and the cruelty of the sketches of human frailty seems less excusable than it did when one swallowed the author's unacknowledged attitudes whole with the book and only felt grateful for this genial Ulsterman and his hard-won confident faith. There is, however, a wise warning from the Teacher in this dream-narrative. Lewis (the narrator) says, 'Could one dare – could one have the face – to go to a bereaved mother, in her misery – when one's not bereaved oneself [and suggest she was being over-possessive of her dead son]?' 'No, no, Son that's no concern of yours. You're not a good enough man for that. When your own heart's been broken it will be time for you to think of talking.' That was truer than Lewis the author could have expected. At his mother's death he had been left feeling that the secure world of childhood had sunk without trace; when his father died, the son was struggling financially as well as spiritually, and certainly was not able to deal with his feelings fully; Mrs Moore's death, in 1951, after a not wholly unhappy life together, in however unusual and difficult circumstances, was the not untimely close of a chapter for her as well as for him. But after that, this man who gave generously and demanded much of his men friends but who was as reticent about his own domestic affairs as he was uninterested in theirs, found his match (more than his match, some would say) in Joy Gresham and, in circumstances quite other than straightforward for a man of his beliefs and reputation, grew up and found an adult love that exacted everything from him and gave him opportunity for growth such as he had never known before. They were married first in a registry office to enable Joy Gresham to remain in the United Kingdom (she was an American), and then by a priest friend who did not refuse to officiate at a marriage involving a divorced person, at what was expected to be her deathbed. Three years later, Joy Lewis did die. It was in loving Joy 'that the essential work of healing mysteriously began'.[9] It took a form which found expression in a book as chaotic and disorderly as the experience itself, and for that very reason, the book was published first under a pseudonym, and, indeed, sales only took off when, after Lewis's death, it was published under his own name.[10]

He refers (I assume) to Charles Williams' death early on:

I had a most vivid feeling of certainty about his continued life; even his enhanced life. I have begged to be given even one hundredth part of the same assurance about H. There is no answer. Only the locked door, the iron curtain, the vacuum, the absolute zero. (p. 11)

Of course his ease in writing did not vanish with grief; but now at last he wrote, at first just to try to save his own sanity, and faced his despairing doubt, not of God's existence but of God's goodness.

The conclusion I dread is not 'So there's no God after all,' but 'So this is what God's really like. Deceive yourself no longer.' (p. 10)

This is the despair at once of the abandoned child and of the truly religious man that Lewis was. He traversed the abyss of bereavement at last, at first hand, no horror left out to which his temperament might expose him. The awful zigzag progress of his grieving was put into words in these few notebooks.

She died. She is dead. Is the word so difficult to learn? (p. 16)

Oh God, God, why did you take such trouble to force this creature out of its shell if it is now doomed to crawl back – to be sucked back – into it? (p. 18)

You never know how much you really believe anything until its truth or falsehood becomes a matter of life and death to you. (p. 21)

Reality, looked at steadily, is unbearable. And how and why did such a reality blossom (or fester) here and there into the terrible phenomenon called consciousness? (p. 25)

I think it is important to notice that the sentiments expressed here are not alien to the C. S. Lewis of his earlier writings. His life, his Ulster Protestant background, his temperamental attraction to dualism, above all the child who remembered the calendar quotation on the day of his mother's death ('Men must endure their going hence') – this is the man who at last faced and lived an intense distress that affected everything he valued.

There were, too, the moments of new perceptiveness (within the bounds of his own limitations) about the relations of the sexes; moments when he realised that sorrow is 'not a state but a process' (p. 47); the moment when the phrase 'She is in God's hand'

gains a new energy when I think of her as a sword. . . . Now perhaps He grasps the hilt; weighs the new weapon; makes lightnings with it in the air. 'A right Jerusalem blade.' (p. 50)

A moment too, describable only in similes, giving a sense of a friend nearby in the dark. He is poised between the two convictions that 'the Eternal Vet is even more inexorable and the possible operations even more painful than all our severest imaginings can forbode' and 'All shall be well, and all shall be well, and all manner of thing shall be well' (p. 51). Finally, he notes the quality of an experience 'of her *mind* momentarily facing my own . . . an extreme and cheerful intimacy' that made 'a sort of spring cleaning in my mind' (pp. 57f.).

All in all, *A Grief Observed* could be called the least dispensable of all Lewis's writings, because it engages with his own experience of grief and loss in a way he had never before been able to do. It is to be hoped that those who still eagerly read the writings of his earlier years read them through the lens of this late piece.

Dorothy L. Sayers

Of the four Anglican writers here being recalled, only Lewis directly wrote of his own experience, and inevitably this autobiographical writing is selective of facts. Dorothy L. Sayers set a firm guard on her own privacy. One can see this as an attitude natural in a novelist who objected to being identified with the point of view of her characters, and natural even in a professional writer who objected to her theological writings being regarded as personal confessions of faith. Arguably her most mature theological writing is in *The Mind of the Maker*,[11] a 'study in the creative mind', and in the Preface to that work she emphasises that she is not pursuing the question of whether 'man' is made in the image of God or God in the image of 'man', but only trying 'to demonstrate that the statements made in the Creeds about the Mind of the Divine Maker represent . . . true statements about the mind of the human maker'. It is as if she clears herself out a space within which she can work freely, putting aside (yet certainly not ignoring) the great questions waiting in the wings.

In a sense it could seem that that is how she responded to the most momentous crisis of her life, the birth of an illegitimate son in 1924. There was to be no marriage to the child's father, and for the whole of her life (for the sake, at first, of her elderly parents) Dorothy Sayers told no one of the son's identity except the cousin who fostered him, the man she later married, who (after some years) adopted him, and, eventually, her son himself. Yet at least part of the inducement to become a successful writer of detective stories was the need to provide financially for her son's upbringing and education. And although Sayers can be believed when she says that an intelligent Zoroastrian could have written one of her earlier articles 'concerning the essentials of Christian doctrine', it is hard to believe that anyone other than a committed orthodox Christian could have published the insights into the creative mind Sayers offers in *The Mind of the Maker*.

One could also, with patience, work out a study of the development of the characters of Harriet Vane and Peter Wimsey in the three novels in which they both have prominent parts that would trace the increasing integration of their lives and characters into the plot until, in the end, the form (the detective story) barely contains them. One could reasonably surmise that this was as far as Dorothy Sayers was willing to expose her own acquaintance with man-woman relationships. In some later short stories Wimsey as detective reverts to his 'flat character' self. Perhaps too in the end she was more deeply interested in 'the mind of the maker'. To look at a *developing* artist pondering the interrelation of the creative Idea, the creative Energy and the creative Power would make an extraordinarily interesting study, not unrelated to the theme of the present book. I would suggest as possible starting-points three quotations from *The Mind of the Maker*:

[T]he artist does not see life as a problem to be solved, but as a medium for creation. (p. 152)

The good that emerges from a conflict of values cannot arise from the total condemnation or destruction of one set of values, but only by the building of a new value, sustained, like an arch, by the tension of the original two. We do not, that is, merely examine the data to disentangle something that was in them already: we use them to construct something that was not there before: neither circumcision nor uncircumcision but a new creature. (p. 155)

[The artist] is not necessarily an artist in handling his personal life, but (since life is the material of his work) he has at least got thus far, that he is using life to create something new. Because of this, the pains and sorrows of this troublesome world can never, for him, be *wholly* meaningless and useless. . . . If, therefore, we are to deal with our 'problems' in 'a creative way', we must deal with them along the artist's lines: not expecting to 'solve' them by a detective trick, but 'to make something of them', even when they are, strictly speaking, unsolvable. (p. 156)

Charles Williams

Charles Williams, the man, the poet, the theologian, the novelist, the stylist and critic, continues to baffle, to attract and to repel in almost equal parts. It is to be hoped that he will one day receive the full-scale sympathetic and critical reassessment that his work deserves. In this chapter I take just one example of his work, from perhaps the most striking of his seven novels, *All Hallows Eve*,[12] published in 1945, the year of his death. It could be cited as recapitulating most of the themes he developed over many years: the doctrine of exchange and of substitution, married love as potential bearer of divine love and truth, and the lure of power over others on grandiose or petty scale.

In the context of the present book, what is striking about *All Hallows Eve* is that it begins with two women, Lester and Evelyn, newly dead as a result of a plane crash in a central London street, and the whole narrative unfolds in their (Christianly viewed) 'Bardo', the gap in which they find, in the place of the newly dead – which is still their own city, experienced in another dimension – what each really wants, and which way she is moving, in relation to those to whom each was closest in her earthly life. Each woman has faults and needs, but the story is one of opportunities for mending of past wrongs, slight things perhaps, but of eternal significance in the light of the mythical-magical plotting by the sinister figure of Simon the Clerk, who seeks control of the worlds both of the dead and of the living through occult means involving the destruction of his own daughter Betty.

If this sounds melodramatic, that is characteristic of all seven novels; in this one the patterning of the exchange of good and of evil is perhaps more skilfully carried out, so that the movement of Lester towards her final taking up into 'all the hallows' is credible at every stage, as is the parallel path of Evelyn towards a bleaker end. Williams is, in fact, one of the few Christian writers who seems able to describe the transitions of the soul towards greater good as plausibly as he does those other movements of decline towards total unthinking acquiescence in evil. This may well be because, as Anne Ridler long ago suggested, the truth at the centre of his teaching, that the whole universe is to be known as good, 'was a truth to him as agonizing as it was inescapable'. Be that as it may, for those who can enjoy Williams' admittedly idiosyncratic style, his preoccupation as a novelist with ideas rather than character, and his pervasive use of magical-occult themes and devices, *All Hallows Eve*, along with *Descent into Hell*, offers a fascinating exposition of the 'progress of the soul' *for* good and ill as well as *through* good and ill.

And others

As a kind of appendix to this chapter, there remain other sources of influence than confessedly Christian writers whose life experiences are reflected in their writings. Turning to a slightly later period of my own life, and asking who were the people who helped to sustain me by their lives or writings, three come to mind at once, a rather strange assortment too (but I do not think that this is uncommon). First was a late discovery of the third book of Vergil's *Aeneid*, with its strong sense of journey-with-a-purpose. Second was Win Ferrier's memoir of her sister Kathleen, an account of a life that I found newly moving and inspiring. What captured my imagination then for the first time was the realisation that great art, like that of the poet or painter or musician or singer, demands not just 'genius' but straightforward patience, dedication and hard work, as well as belief in one's own capacities. The realisation that the artist too has a wilderness to cross, a way to find and a path to follow came to me strangely late, perhaps, but usefully. And so far from defining a 'gap' of immeasurable size between religious and artistic pursuits, my perception of Ferrier's life (and her early death too) opened up ways of connection between different human callings. My horizons were widened. The gap may remain, but it is one to be explored, leaving behind some preconceptions and expecting insights on the way.

Last in this revisiting some of those with whom I have travelled for parts of my own journey is the poet Edwin Muir, whom I place here among the artists, a man shot through (by his own account) with belief in God and the immortality of the soul. He wrote of a time in 1939 when 'I had a vague sense . . . that Christ was the turning-point of time and the meaning of life to everyone, no matter what his conscious beliefs . . .'.[13]

He described memorably the security of his Orkney childhood, despite the declining fortunes of his farming family. T. S. Eliot wrote of 'the sensibility of the remote islander, the boy from a simple offshore community who then plunged into the sordid horror of industrialism in Glasgow, who struggled to understand the modern world of the metropolis in London, and finally the realities of central Europe in Prague where he and his wife . . . saw the Iron Curtain fall'.

Muir himself wrote of his early years:

> The farmers did not know ambition and the petty torments of ambition; they did not realize what competition was, though they lived at the end of Queen Victoria's reign; they helped one another with their work when help was required, following the old usage; they had a culture made up of legend, folk-song, and the poetry and prose of the Bible; they had customs which sanctioned their instinctive feelings for the earth; their life was an order, and a good order. So that when my father and mother

left Orkney for Glasgow when I was fourteen, we were plunged out of order into chaos. We did not know it at the time, and I did not realize it for many years after I had left Glasgow. My father and mother and two of my brothers died in Glasgow within two years of one another. Four members of our family died there within two years. That is a measure of the violence of the change. (p. 63)

Not until a stay in Dresden in 1922 did Muir find that:

I seemed at last to recover from that long illness that had seized me when, at fourteen, I came to Glasgow. I realized that I must live over again the years which I had lived wrongly, and that everyone should live his life twice, for the first attempt is always blind. I went over my life in that resting space, like a man who after travelling a long, featureless road suddenly realizes that, at this point or at that, he had noticed almost without knowing it, with the corner of his eye, some rare treasure, yet in his sleep-walking had gone on, consciously aware only of the blank road flowing back beneath his feet. These objects, like Griseldas, were still patiently waiting at the points where I had first ignored them, and my full gaze could take in things which an absent glance had once passed over unseeingly, so that life I had wasted was returned to me. . . . In living that life over again I struck up a first acquaintance with myself. (pp. 192–3)

It was the moment of discovery that awakened his imagination and, at thirty-five, he began to write poetry. Not surprisingly, biblical images, as well as those of European literature, are common in his poetry.

> Forty years this burning
> Circuitous path, feet spurning
> The sliding sand and turning
> The wheel, turning again

Sharp rock, soft dust, a land
Choked in sand.

Once in the wilderness
A stream leapt from the smitten rock, flowed on,
flowed on, and then
The rock was sealed again,
Our hearts were dry again.
Since then we have marched through emptiness
Over the sea-ground of the sealess plain.[14]

The penultimate verse ends 'Where is our land?' and the poem itself concludes:

There is a stream
We have been told of. Where it is
We do not know. But it is not a dream,
Though like a dream. We cannot miss
The road that leads us to it. Fate
Will take us there that keeps us here.
Neither hope nor fear
Can hasten or retard the date
Of our deliverance; when we shall leave this sand
And enter the unknown and feared and longed-for land.

The last poem of his collected works (second edition) returns to images derived from his Orkney childhood, ending:

All things stand in their place
Till hatred beats them down,
Furies and fantasies
Strike flat the little town.
Then all rise up again,
But heart and blood and bone,
The very stones in the street,
Roof and foundation stone,
Remember and foreknow.

Memories, prophecies,
The song the ploughman sings,
The simple dream of peace,
Dark dreams in the dead of night
And on the reckless brow
Bent to let chaos in,
Tell that they shall come down,
Be broken, and rise again.[15]

From such experience, such creative work, are spun the many-coloured threads of wisdom that can guide those who take them up through the wilderness-maze of everyday life.

6
Women in the Wilderness

The concept of liminality gives us a way of understanding and talking about the process of change, whether personal change or some sort of social change. In the next three chapters we want to look in some detail at one particular example of a group of people in transition and see what an understanding of liminality offers in terms of being able to make the most creative use of the time of transition.

We wanted to write in this section about something from our own experience, that is, to speak from within a time and place of transition. There are several areas of change which we could have chosen to write about; after all, we live in a much changing world and many of us are involved in fairly major life changes more than one at a time. To some extent we can choose change; more often than not, it seems to choose us. On a very personal level we both experienced a good deal of change as we left our respective religious orders – Hannah an active order after nine years, Jennifer an enclosed contemplative order after twenty-seven years. Although it is now several years since we left, neither of us would say that we are totally through the transition. That particular change involves most obviously loss of family community, home, economic security and source of income, occupational identity, faith community, and neighbourhood. Transition has to take place within each of these aspects of change *and* as a whole in relation to personal identity: it is about some very practical matters like finding somewhere to live, and it is also about enormous emotional and spiritual upheaval.

The second experience we could perhaps have written about is that of the current state of traditional religious life, by which we mean active and contemplative religious orders in both Anglican and Roman Catholic Churches. At a recent seminar one of us ran for vocation and formation directors from Catholic communities, after an introduction to this model of change, those taking part were keen to discuss where they thought their orders were in relation to the liminal experience of transition. Recognising that individuals and particular households may be in quite different places with regard to change, they nevertheless felt it was possible to have a sense of the history of the order as a whole and where in its history it might be now. There was some agreement that the creative way forward may be to let go of a great deal of the known and tried in order to allow radical new possibilities for the future. To some extent this is what happened as a result of Vatican II. Religious life in the Anglican Church has suffered from having no similar obligatory shake-up. But religious orders seem to be in another phase: most of them do not have new members joining, at least not on a permanent basis, and it has become increasingly difficult for many of them to continue to run the houses and projects (schools, community centres, hostels, etc.) which have been central to their lives. It would seem necessary to make some fundamental changes – or, rather, to allow such changes the possibility of taking place. The model of change we have outlined may give some clues as to what that process might involve, not least the necessity of considerable and real loss and of a time in the wilderness of not knowing what the future will bring.

This leads us on to consider the experience of transition we would like to look at in some detail in the chapters which follow. It is the experience of a growing number of women who no longer find a positive place, or any place at all, within the Christian churches. Although we are ourselves Christian feminists, women who experience a sense of loss and alienation in relation to the churches are from a range of backgrounds and perspectives and not all by any means would describe themselves as feminist. The thing which we tend to have in common is that it is our sense of being *a woman* which leads to a corresponding loss of the sense of the church as a creative spiritual home.

In what follows we begin by identifying further the women we are referring to; we look at where we are in relation to the liminality model we have already outlined; and we ask what clues the model gives us as to how we can make the most of the time and place in which we find ourselves.

We believe that by looking at one example which involves both individual and group transition, we can demonstrate just how creative the concept of liminality could be in helping us through processes of vital change. We have chosen this example because we can speak out of our own experience and from within our own community, that of Christian feminists. We hope that those of you who are in transition, but in different places and within different communities or no community, will nevertheless see parallels in the journey and will translate the use of the model to your own situations.

In a recent mailing of 'Women In Theology' (WIT),[1] a Christian feminist network, there are three-and-a-half pages of events listed. Most of them are advertising forthcoming meetings of Christian women gathering to do theology – in its broadest sense. Titles include: Feminist spirituality: imaging a new reality; Women, Nature and God; Women and Men – What's the problem?; Women and Power – What is Feminist Theology?; Equal Rites; Women-Church; Rescuing Sexuality from Fundamentalism; Women Transforming Images of Christ; Partners in Priesthood; Distorted Images: Christianity and Pornography; Liberating Women – New Theological Directions; Feminism and Christian Ethics; Images of Women in Church and Society; Theology of Desire.

Elsewhere in the mailing there is news from Women In Theology groups in various parts of Britain, each with its own programme, as well as reviews of some of the growing number of theological books written by women, and news of a new university course which combines social and pastoral theology with feminist studies.

This was the WIT mailing, but we might just as well have been reading the newsletter of the Catholic Women's Network (CWN), or a number of other groups concerned with women and the churches. Who could doubt that there is an issue about being a woman in the church? Or in Christianity itself?

An important feature of women's groups who gather to do theology, or worship together, is the diversity of the positions of the women present in relation to the church. For most women such groups do not represent an alternative to church membership in some form, but what Rosemary Ruether calls a 'liberated zone'. Whether as priests working in parish ministry, or as occasional visitors to Sunday eucharist, women spend much of their time in church fighting feelings of anger, boredom and the desire to walk out and never come back. Church structures and hierarchies (evident at any parish eucharist), liturgies which make the experience, and very existence, of women invisible, and images of God more often than not as a regal male tyrant, all contribute to depression or rage and a headache by Sunday lunch. To spend time with other women (and sometimes also men) who share similar feelings, without having continuously to fight some sort of personal ground, is real liberation and relief.

Groups of this kind that we are a part of typically include women who work full time for the church, those who have been actively involved in local churches all their lives and who continue to be so, those who walked out of the church years ago and have no intention of going back, and those who (sometimes against their 'better' judgement) hang on in their denominational church but do not regularly attend parish worship. Christians, post-Christians, and sometimes those who may not want to define themselves in relation to Christianity at all, share the desire to engage in a theology and spiritual search which makes women's experience central.

What kind of wilderness?

As we said earlier in the book, Christian feminists are among those who tend to use the image of wilderness to describe aspects of their spiritual journey. To understand something of the nature of *this* wilderness experience we want to look first at the Southwark Wilderness Liturgy (see Appendix).

Although the Southwark liturgy took place some years ago now, it was published in *Celebrating Women*[2] and parts of it continue to be used in women's liturgies. Its symbolism is powerful and gives us an idea of the nature and the agenda of women's journeys in this particular wilderness. We want to pick out four themes of the liturgy to describe further the experiences of many women in and around the churches. They are *struggle, remembrance, nourishment* and *commitment*.

Struggle

First, we are engaged in a struggle. To be more precise, we are engaged in lots of struggles, but we can probably see three overlapping levels or perspectives of 'the struggle'. They are all evident in the Southwark liturgy: the *personal* struggle of an individual's spiritual journey; the struggle of a group *against* unjust laws and practices of an institution, in this case the church; the struggle *with* other groups who suffer other kinds of oppression and injustice.

The personal struggle, although obviously the most immediate, is often the most difficult to articulate. In the Southwark liturgy, where the focus is the injustice of the church's refusal to ordain women, the struggle is essentially combative and corporate. But it was nevertheless created by individuals struggling to find a language, in words, symbols and images, to express a vital part of their faith experience.

The personal struggle of a Christian feminist begins with

the same question facing any Christian: how can I live faithfully? The churches claim to be able to give us an answer and also the things we need – doctrine, theology, synodical government, papal infallibility, parishes, the ASB, confession, *Faith in the City*, Vatican II, The Methodist Hymn Book . . . to name but a few – but some of us find there more obstacles than sources of inspiration. We are forced to look elsewhere for many of the resources to help us live in a way that seems to us faithful to the gospel and to our religious journey.

Liturgy is central. Most women who feel alienated from the churches experienced that alienation first through Sunday worship. Reasons for this sense of alienation may be an all-male priesthood or ministry, the invisibility of women in the language ('for us men and for our salvation'), the imaging of God as exclusively male, a dualism which rejects the bodily (especially if it is a female body), or a more general sense that the shape and style of the liturgy is just all 'wrong'.

Women who feel this way need either to struggle to make some sort of sense of their church's worship and their reason for continuing to attend it, or they must struggle to create some kind of alternative. For many women, it is clear what does not work or does not have meaning liturgically; but it is far less clear what the alternatives are. We find ourselves continually on new ground which is both exciting and extraordinarily hard work. We are forced to do our own theology, envision what it means to us to be church, create liturgies which express our deepest desires and concerns, build bases from which to do these things; and all this not with the churches' help, but more often than not with a considerable amount of condemnation and mockery.

One such group that formed consciously to work and worship together (women and men) to create inclusive liturgies is the St Hilda Community, formerly based in East London. Some of their liturgies have been formally eucharistic, with a woman priest or minister 'presiding', while others have not relied on the presence of an ordained person. Those who attend take responsibility for preparing the worship and its style varies: sometimes new prayers are written; on other occasions, prayers, readings, songs, are gathered from a variety of sources and shaped into a liturgy. It is recognisably 'church' and in many ways fairly conservative experimental worship. Nevertheless, when an established Christian publisher published a book about the St Hilda Community[3] which included some of the prayers and liturgies they used, there was uproar in the press. Headlines included 'Feminist Interference', 'How dare these busybodies re-write Christ', and 'Prayer "heresy" '. The prayer singled out for most attention is a version of the Lord's Prayer by Jim Cotter,[4] first published some years ago, which begins 'Beloved, our Father and Mother, in whom is heaven'. Churchmen described it as 'heretical', 'totally unnecessary and foolish', an attempt to 'subvert Christianity', and 'blasphemous'. An Anglican bishop lashed out at the publishers: 'It's an act of madness and will not be taken seriously – a very limited piece of liberal thinking, more a comment on the Godforsaken nature of our society, not God himself. They're publishers and the first aim of publishers is to make money. You shouldn't muck about with God's word.'

The honest and sincere struggle of these Christians to find more inclusive and appropriate liturgies is even more viciously written off in a feature article in the *Daily Mail*:

> The new prayer book . . . refers to the deity as God the Lover and God the Womb-Bearer. It conjures up a nightmare vision not so much of a Goddess, but of an unlovable God the Ms. who takes a degree in feminist studies, refuses to 'honour and obey' her husband, divorces him, raises a one-parent family, is an expert on contraception and abortions, becomes a managing director and ends up as God the Lesbian.[5]

One is left speechless. All that because a small group of Christian men and women used a prayer which imaged God as female as well as male – and (significantly) because an established religious publisher published it.

Our point is that the struggle of women (and obviously men) to create new liturgies, and to make visible and central women's experience in the doing of theology, is also a struggle against enormous prejudice and sexism in church and in society.

Remembrance

The Wilderness Liturgy at Southwark includes a good deal of remembering: our foremothers in the Bible; women who have faced the unknown in faith; the great reformers of history; those who have struggled ahead of us to make the church a more just and equal community of faith. This remembering is first of all a calling up. We are not alone in our struggle for justice: indeed it is no new struggle. Countless women before us have been in their own wilderness, fighting just the same kinds of battles against prejudice and injustice. The liturgy recalls their courage, seeks their prayers, and reminds us that the path has been trodden before.

The remembering is also a making visible. Making sure that women remain largely invisible in the liturgy is one effective way of maintaining the patriarchal *status quo*. An all-male priesthood is one obvious way of keeping women invisible: the procession into Canterbury Cathedral at the enthronement of George Carey was a spectacular visual of Church of England leadership. All very well to say, as was said at the time, that just because women could not be priests did not mean they could not exercise leadership in the church – we are not fooled.

A less obvious invisibility is reflected, for example, in the very unequal commemorations of male and female saints in the church's calendar. We have to dig much deeper to uncover the heroic stories of Christian women down the centuries. Women's history gets buried beneath layers of patriarchal trivialisation and dismissiveness, not least within the churches. We need to find and tell their stories, and keep reading aloud the stories of women in the Bible.

The third aspect of remembering is the remembrance of the painfulness of the struggle – the awfulness of how it sometimes feels and the temptation to despair of change. Although it is paralysing to get stuck in that remembrance, it is necessary to acknowledge it if we are to move on to a more creative energy. In her excellent book, *Despair and Personal Power in the Nuclear Age*,[6] Joanna Macy demonstrates how a facing of the dark together, with a willingness to acknowledge and experience pain, can lead to a deep bondedness and ability to face challenges that lie ahead with new courage and energy.

Nourishment

The wilderness for Christian women is also a place in which to seek nourishment. Many women we talk to use the language of hunger and starvation to describe their experience of liturgical worship: they remain unfed by the diet on offer at their local church; or, having left that, they feel starved of corporate worship altogether. The church feeds with the bread and wine of communion, but also with symbols, images, gestures. If these are experienced as alienating or oppressive we feel hungry and sick. Strong words, but so are the words of the liturgy.

So in the wilderness women must seek to be fed. They look for the nourishment of community, of shared vision and struggle, for the recognition of meaningful images and symbols to express their journey of faith. In the Southwark liturgy they share milk and honey cake as symbols of their ability to feed one another, and in remembrance of that earlier community as it journeyed to the Promised Land.

Commitment

Where you go, I will go, and where you stay, I will stay. Your people shall be my people, and your God my God. Where you die, I will die, and there I will be buried. I swear a solemn oath before Yahweh your God: nothing but death shall divide us. (Ruth 1:16–18)

The Wilderness Liturgy is a corporate act of worship and

witness. This wilderness community includes not only those present outside the cathedral, but also all those women named or spoken of in the intercessions and thanksgivings. We commit ourselves to each other because this is not a journey we want to make alone, and we know that it is going to take a lot of us to change the world.

Our commitment is not only to our sisters and brothers in this particular struggle, but to all 'the hurt, the disadvantaged and the alienated'. But perhaps most poignantly the commitment is to be *here* and to stay *here* – here in this wilderness of having left but not arrived, of having lost much and found little.

> Shall a woman bear a child without pains? Give birth to a son before the onset of labour? Who has heard of anything like this? Who has seen any such thing? Shall a country be born after one day's labour, shall a nation be brought to birth all in a moment? But Zion, at the onset of her pangs, bore her children. Shall I bring to the point of birth and not deliver? (Isaiah 66:7–9)

We are right back in the liminal, in the gap between what has been and what is yet to be.

7

A Place Transfigured

I recognize that the great advantage bestowed upon me by my marginal situation was that it was also an opportunity. It had the potential to become liminal – that is, to be a threshold to Other and New perceptions.[1]

The place referred to in the chapter title is the place of change, the place of being between one thing and another, the place that is both exciting and terrifying. It is a place we have also called wilderness.

The wilderness is the untamed, the uncultivated, the life-giving, life-restoring place without which the planet's eco-system would collapse. Similarly, without spaces of wildness we would shrivel and die, inwardly if not physically.

We have identified wilderness as a time and place of transition, the 'pivotal moment that has no movement of itself, but allows movement to take place'. We have looked, with the help of psychological and anthropological perspectives, at the power of this time and place and of those who dwell there.

People who reside on boundaries effect change beyond the particular changes they themselves are involved in. This means that they represent a threat to those concerned with social or group order and the definition of whatever or who-ever is within the boundary on which they dwell. Those who live on the boundaries of the institutional churches are therefore particularly instigators of change and renewal. Paradoxically, the boundary will not be the creative place of change for them or for the institution unless they can leave behind or let go of what has become dead or oppressive for them. This movement from margin to threshold, from victim to prophet was poignantly described by Bridget Rees in a sermon to the congregation at St Matthew's, Brixton in 1986. We include a fairly lengthy extract from that sermon because it illustrates so well both the need to leave behind and the cost of doing so.

A few weeks ago the General Synod of the Church of England decided to refuse to allow women priests lawfully ordained overseas to celebrate the Eucharist in Churches in England. Male priests from overseas of course continue to be welcome. At the same synod, though it was agreed women could become deacons, the ordination of women to the priesthood was postponed yet again despite the agreement of several years ago that there is no fundamental objection to the ordination of women to the priesthood.

I decided that I had sat down by the waters of Babylon and wept for long enough. Enough is enough. I am taking down my harp from the trees and I am playing it. I am singing the Lord's song even if it is in a strange land.

I love the Church of England. It has been part and parcel of my life since I was born. My father is and my mother's father was an Anglican priest. I was paid to work for the Church of England for fourteen years. I have taught, I have preached, I have helped train future priests (male priests). I have over and over again worked to change the Church from within; I have believed what I have been told over and over again, that the only way to change something is from inside. But enough is enough.

Just as the Hebrews in Egypt decided enough was enough, I and many women are deciding enough is enough. We do not have to go on and on being victims, we do not have to go on allowing ourselves to be oppressed, we do not have to go on allowing ourselves to be depressed. We no longer need to hang up our harps.

Three years ago thirteen women left Southwark Cathedral just after receiving communion at an ordination service – we left to celebrate a wilderness liturgy outside the cathedral. We were enacting a decision to go into the wilderness, to leave the oppression of Egypt behind, to refuse to continue to be victims. It was around that time that I stopped working for the Church of England. Since then, although I have never been to an ordination service, I have continued to worship, receive and administer communion and preach in Anglican churches. Though I have been in the wilderness I have received from and have kept connections with the oppressors. A month ago I decided that I could no longer continue to receive communion from male priests in a church which continues to oppress women so badly, a church which refuses to test my or any other woman's vocation to the priesthood in the way that it tests men's.

I began to question my own vocation (even more than I always do). Perhaps God is calling me more to a prophetic than a priestly ministry? Most of the prophets were on the edge, on the outside, over against the institution. Perhaps this is my vocation, at least for the moment.

Not receiving communion makes the wilderness more of a wilderness in some senses. I have found it very painful on three occasions, not receiving communion with my friends and fellow Anglicans; I shall find it particularly difficult this morning [Bridget was a member of this congregation]. But I want to claim life. I do not want to go on being a victim. I do not want to go on pretending, hiding and suppressing my feelings, my beliefs. It is hard to turn my back on an organization, on a community of people I love, but it is harder to go on living a lie. I want to witness in my not receiving communion to the brokenness of our community, to make this visible rather than pretend that everything is all right.[2]

How do we move from margin to threshold? And having done so, how do we harness the creative potential of this liminal wilderness and limit its disintegrative forces? We suggest there is a process which looks something like this:

- *Recognise the crisis.*
  'I believe, but I cannot believe *that*.'
  'Going to church gives me a headache.'
  'I have faith, but it's not the faith of my "fathers".'
  'I want to leave the church, but what could I do, where could I go? I still feel I'm a Christian.'
  'I haven't a clue where I'm going any more in a religious sense.'
  'I know *something* is important to me, but I've lost a language to describe it.'
  'I feel as if God, the church, the whole lot has just died on me.'

- *Recognise the vision or hope that is in you.*
  A sense of crisis is very often felt because of a positive flip-side to this otherwise negative experience. Frustration with the church, for example, is frustration because I have a vision that it does not have to be like this. The community of faith *could* be more open, more adventurous, more relevant. So, what do I hope for? What do I believe is really important? What values do I want to try to live by and how do I want to express them? Do I want to do this with other people who share a similar vision? What is the experience which makes me feel that all this *matters*?

- *Acknowledge the loss.*
  What do I both want and fear to lose? A worshipping community? Some old and formerly cherished beliefs? A particular image of God? A place and identity within my local church? My job? My vocation?

- *Say goodbye.*
  Try to discern what you need to let go of on this journey

of transition and, either on your own or with a small group, participate in some simple ritual of letting go and leaving behind (see p. 113).

- *Create some initial boundaries.*
If you have left a local church, you may find the regular worshipping time on Sunday mornings a real loss. For the hour or so when you would have been in church, set the same time aside for listening to music, going for a walk, meditating, cooking something special – whatever nourishes your soul. Rather than just the hour a week on Sunday, you may want to set some time aside each day in this way. What is important, if it is to provide a sense of boundary and containment at this time of change, is that it is a fixed time and it has priority. You may also want to do some study – perhaps theology that clarifies your own ideas – or write down some of your own reflections. In setting time aside like this you are creating a part of the new container for your religious faith and experience – and you are taking your journey seriously.

- *Build community.*
There is a depressing privatisation of spirituality which mirrors the extreme individualism and egocentricity of western cultures. To think and talk only of 'my journey' and never of 'our journey' is to miss, if not the whole point, then certainly a major part of the point of any religious quest. If there is no *meeting* at the level of faith, it is hard to see how it can be faith at all.

'I miss the chance to be quiet with other women and just sit and contemplate. It's just not the same if you do it on your own.'[3] The woman quoted here is describing that sense of meeting.

One of the greatest losses we hear expressed is that of a worshipping community, usually when a person has left a local congregation. The human desire to belong is very strong and churches often provide a sense of community, especially in otherwise rather impersonal cities.

Rosemary Ruether's book *Women-Church* offers a model for a new faith community that is fairly demanding of its members in their commitment.[4] Our own experience indicates that women in the wilderness of exodus and transition from patriarchal religion are quite ambivalent about community, both wanting a sense of belonging and others to share liturgy with, but also being wary (on a practical if not a theoretical level) of precise or ongoing commitment. This may be a sign of the inability to let go and move into the wilderness which we have been talking about, or it may be the desire for some breathing space after a lot of previous church community battles. It may also be that only when there are some committed alternative communities in existence will women (and others) feel able and free to leave existing communities. One senses, in the inability to face the task of building community, the presence of the depression and lack of energy that often mark the process of grieving. One of our hardest obstacles in setting up a spirituality resource centre for women in London was, despite huge enthusiasm for the idea, the lack of belief that such a project was possible. We opened the doors earlier than might have been 'sensible' because we knew we had to convince women that it really was happening. Somehow we had to make visible the possibility of the 'Active Boundary Living' described in the next chapter.

8
'Active Boundary Living'

'In that Future time, my marginality would be transformed into Active Boundary Living.'[1]

It is not enough to hold an ideology of criticism and social analysis as an interpretive base, nor to participate in protest and action groups and organizations as vehicles of change. One needs communities of nurture to guide one through death to the old symbolic order of patriarchy to rebirth into a new community of being and living. One needs not only to engage in rational theoretical discourse about this journey, one also needs deep symbols and symbolic actions to guide and interpret the actual experience of the journey from sexism to liberated humanity.[2]

Women-church embraces a liminal religiosity. It does not claim to have an original 'true' faith that can be revived in the style of the Reformation. Nor does it claim to know the shape of the future. It stands on two thresholds, looking backward to options in biblical and prebiblical faiths that were hinted at but probably never developed, and looking forward to new possibilities whose shape is unclear. It does not repudiate all that has gone on in between, but it seeks to appropriate its best insights as material for a new future.[3]

So writes Rosemary Radford Ruether in her book *Women-Church*. The book named a movement which was already under way, albeit not an easy one to define. The 'intentional communities of faith and worship' which Ruether writes about are many and varied; some have a definite sense of themselves as 'women-church', others do not. But it is important to understand at the outset that, for many of those who are a part of it, women-church does not represent an 'alternative' church. A large number of women who are members of these kinds of groups are also faithful (if unhappy) members of the historical churches. Indeed, Ruether is clear in her argument for a dialectical relationship between historical institution and spirit-filled community:

> The basic assumption of this book is that the church cannot be defined only as historical institution or only as spirit-filled community. Rather, the church exists as a dialectical interaction between the two elements. But the relationship between the two has been constantly misdefined, usually by the historical institution, but at times by the renewal community as well. And so the relationship breaks down into repression and separation. Seldom does the interplay between the two take place with optimal creativity. (p. 32)

One of our suggestions in this book is that the spirit-filled community is a liminal community; it dwells on the threshold and threatens change, which in turn represents both opportunity and danger. One thing institutions fear more than anything else is dis-order, and you cannot change without the cards being shuffled, as it were. Anyone who sat through the Church of England General Synod's debates on the ordination of women to the priesthood could not help being aware of the number of times the phrase 'threat to the order of . . .' was used by opponents of the measure.

However, women-church exists not perhaps primarily to change the historic institution, but (like any church) because of the needs of its members.

Thus the first step in forming the feminist exodus from patriarchy is to gather women together to articulate their own experience and communicate it with each other. Women assure each other that they are not crazy, that they really have been defined and confined by systemic marginalization, and they learn how to recognize and resist the constant messages from patriarchal culture that try to enforce their acquiescence and collaboration with it. Distressing as it may seem to males who imagine themselves sympathetic to feminism, this process of consciousness raising must necessarily have a separatist stage. Women have to withdraw from male-dominated spaces so they can gather together and define their own experience [p. 59] ... Women-church is the Christian theological expression of this stage of feminist collectivization of women's experience and the formation of critical culture.

As we said earlier, women-church is hard to define. Ruether is careful in her book (see note 4 of the Introduction) to distinguish between terms, and here we use the term 'women-church' to describe the contemporary movement, recognising that it is made up of small groups of women, informal networks, annual conferences and summer schools, individuals, more formal organisations, and so on. In the USA there have been several annual women-church gatherings; there has been nothing comparable in the UK, but that does not mean that women-church does not exist here: it certainly does.

Women-church and the experience of liminality

An important part of women-church is the building of community; not a rigidly defined in-group, but nevertheless something to which it is possible to 'belong', to be a part of, to be involved with. If women-church is a response to women's needs, why is the need to belong now so important?

Women-church is an exodus community in the sense that women are in exodus from patriarchy, in particular from a patriarchal church which has marginalised women and women's experience. Some of those women who make up women-church are also much involved in local parish churches, or in working for national church organisations. Others reluctantly still 'go to church', but with a considerable sense of alienation and concern that they may in fact be damaging their souls. Others again have ceased to belong in any sense to a local or national denominational church.

For women in each of these groups there is inevitably an experience of loss: of worshipping community, of belief, of spiritual nourishment, of being on good terms with the vicar, of friends, perhaps even of job. To be in *ex*odus is to be leaving. Even if it is a leaving of something oppressive it still frequently involves the experience of loss. Even if I hate Sunday worship at my local church, it gives me something to hate. Better to have a brick wall to bash one's head against rather than nowhere to rest one's head. Or so we might often feel.

We began this book with reference to homelessness: the wilderness as the place of journeying rather than arrival. Our involvement in the women-church movement, where we have shared stories with many women, has shown us just how deep is the experience of loss and a kind of 'spiritual homelessness'. Equally significant is the silence that seems to surround the experience of loss, although it is perhaps less deafening now than it has been. There may well be a sense that the exodus journey *must* be exciting, challenging, utterly worthwhile, something for which we must be strong and resolute, certain in our rejection of the (patriarchal) church.

But it isn't like that. Consider Rosie Miles' recent book, *Not in Our Name: Voices of Women who have left the Church.*[4] It is a matter for rejoicing that these women have finally been given a voice (and that in a book published by an official Church of England body), but it is noticeable that a number of the women clearly have not actually left the church. They deeply resent the church, and certainly do not feel at home in it, but they have not *left*.

Another example. At a weekend workshop on women and

the church, the (male) facilitator began by asking us to arrange a large room the way we would want it for worship. He had brought along a number of 'props' – candle, Bible, lectern, chalice, stole, etc. – which we were asked to place. The whole exercise was to be done in silence and it was pointed out we would need to negotiate with each other. Out of the thirty or so participants there were about six of us who instantly headed out of the room, through the glass doors and into the garden. We had all decided we did not want to 'play church'. But what was really interesting was that only one or two of those six wandered off deeper into the garden; the rest of us hung around the doorway and watched what was going on inside. Every now and then we might wander a few yards further away, but each time came back and peered once more through the window.

That exercise provided a vivid image of where many women find themselves in relation to the church. They can no longer bear to be inside, and many do not want to be bothered merely to try to rearrange the furniture. But neither can they, nor do they want to, leave altogether. Instead, in one way or another, they hang around the porch.

Now, the porch, the churchyard and, most poignantly, the lychgate, all represent parts of the physical boundary between the church and 'the world'. In a physical sense, there is no fine line marking 'in' the church (as place) and 'out' of the church. There are churches, usually in towns and cities, where you step straight through the door on to the pavement, but even these often have some kind of vestibule (which may contain service books, notice boards or a book stall). It is as if we instinctively need some 'in-between' space between church and world, 'sacred' and 'profane'.

The reason for pausing to reflect on church architecture and geography is that it gives us quite a powerful image about where many of us find ourselves. We are not 'in' the church, and we are not 'out'. We do not feel as if we really belong, and yet we have not left. We may feel acutely the tension of having one foot in and one foot out. We may experience a sense of being both in and out, at the same time as feeling neither in nor out. Our position is ambivalent: our place is liminal: we stand on the threshold.

This is, of course, an image. We do not literally hang around the churchyard. We may indeed be sitting in a pew every Sunday, yet have a strong sense of not belonging. Or we may have had little to do formally with the church for a long time, yet still feel, strongly but reluctantly, a part of it.

If the threshold position is ours, then we are in the kind of liminal, or transitional, wilderness we have been describing in this book. We are faced with the dangers and opportunities, the ambivalences, of any liminal state. How are we to 'guard the chaos' within this phase of our religious journey? How do we cherish and nourish the creative opportunity, whilst containing the threat of disintegration and 'lostness'?

If we return to the image of the church and churchyard (with porch and lychgate), we could imagine two scenarios – and we have heard many women's stories which make both a reality.

The first: the churchyard is full of rather tense and tired women, some looking constantly towards the building, others gathered firmly around the porch, looking longingly to the hills beyond the lychgate. Some wish they could be happily inside singing their favourite hymns, just as they were a year or two ago. Others long to be free of it all, to leave it all behind, but somehow they just do not seem to manage it. Is it the worship that stops them, or the community they have belonged to for so long, or is it just habit? Who knows? Most of the women, however, are more aware of what has been important to them rather than what is important now, or how it might all be in the future.

The second scenario: the churchyard (which is a big one!) resembles a camp site (it probably even contains tents once pitched at Greenham). There are women everywhere, looking as though they are having a good time. Some sing together, others chat around the fire. One group is looking rather earnest as they eat a late breakfast together. There is laughter here, and there are tears; there is the buzz of conversation, and waves of silence. Every now and then a woman wanders up to one of the church windows to see what is going on inside and who is there today. As the congregation comes out, some stay and talk and swell the numbers for lunch. (Some, of course, including the current vicar, look utterly disapprovingly at the camp site; they cannot understand how the bishop came to lose the court case over the eviction.) The lunch party grows still further as small groups of women come to join them out of the hills. As Sunday afternoon rolls by the debates and the laughter get louder.

In the first scenario the churchyard represents the margin, and the women there represent those who have been marginalised by the institutional church. They feel lost and powerless. They may have been told that the margin is the place of the prophet, but they are wearied by years of being prophetic. Their energy has been drained by their focus on the church; rarely do they receive visits from the hills, and there is just not time or energy to spare to go there themselves.

In the second scenario the churchyard represents the threshold. It is a meeting place. Some of the women live here – perhaps only for relatively short periods, although some have always lived here – while others drop in for lunch, for a chat, for rituals, for the storytelling that is always a feature of life here. At any one moment, the collection of women gathered at the camp is a wonderful mixture. There are rows and there are tears, there is laughter and rejoicing; all the ups and downs of life are found and held within the camp.

This second scenario is our vision for women-church, an attempt to establish a 'home' in the place of 'no-home', so that those who are called or driven there by the Spirit may be held and contained while they explore further the meaning and purposes of God.

Of course there are limitations to the image on offer. But the point we want to make is that this space, this experience of being neither in nor out (and both) can be a place to enjoy and a place in which to create new things and weave new ideas. It is a place of separation *and* a place of meeting; it is therefore a place of change. Those who live on this threshold provide a meeting place where labels of 'insider' and 'outsider' are left at the doors.

With all its limitations, one of the things this image still offers is a clear picture of how those who occupy liminal space effect change. It is as if by standing on the threshold they keep a door open (or create a passageway) between one side of the boundary and the other, allowing people and ideas to cross backwards and forwards. This is the way in which the threshold community in our example aids the renewal of the historic institution. It is also the reason for its being a threat: it makes it much more difficult to define clearly who is in and who is out, thus threatening the institution's identity and order. Members of the threshold community (and membership is very fluid) do not have to be constantly focusing their attention on the institution, shaking their fists or banging their heads against its walls; they simply have to live on its boundaries and keep the door open, providing a gathering place that is everyone's place and no one's place. We may well spend some of our time shaking our proverbial fists, naming injustice, and so on, but we can also effect change by partying there with a whole mixture of party guests.

In order to illustrate further what we mean by this threshold space, we would like now to describe briefly two projects we have been involved in which we believe in their own ways represent attempts at creating threshold community.

Womenspace

When we left our religious communities we had the dream of setting up a women's 'retreat' centre. This was partly because we had seen and experienced the value of women's religious space. (It is extraordinary, incidentally, how men and women who have a very 'high' view of traditional women's religious communities have the strongest and most negative reactions to other forms of women-only space, even when it is created for a religious purpose.) However, at the time of leaving, we were both homeless, jobless and without savings. Then was not the moment to set about trying to raise hundreds of thousands of pounds, or trying to persuade some unknown benefactor to part with a large house in a beautiful part of the countryside. Instead, we found ourselves temporary accommodation, got our former convent (ever supportive) to print some headed notepaper, and launched our 'business', 'Ward and Wild Research and Editorial Services' (which the postman said sounded like a comedy double-act!).

We mention this rather personal bit of Womenspace's history because we think it bears witness to the real difficulty of helping to create threshold community: you cannot do it if you are safely and securely tucked up in an institutional job.

Anyway, we were now ready to start something and to move this way or that as opportunities arose. We wanted an opportunity to meet with other women around issues of religion and spirituality. We had had enough of the internal politics of organised women's community and did not feel we wanted to take on any kind of formal 'group'. With an eye still on a future permanent base of some kind for women, we were also interested in testing the water to see if women from in and around the churches wanted to meet in women-only space.

So, we set up Womenspace, now in its sixth year. We gave it that name because we did not want anything that sounded as organised as 'women-church', and the word 'space' expressed both our commitment to making a physical space and to the desire for 'spaciness'. The place we chose to meet in was an Anglican Franciscan community house where Hannah had lived for three-and-a-half years and whose members we knew well. It has a beautiful sitting room which can be combined with the equally beautiful and simple chapel to make one large and very comfortable meeting space. Two ironical factors in this choice of Womenspace venue were that the house was an all-male household at the time – the brothers very hospitably and generously staying well out of the way while we were there – and the fact that the house is actually owned by the Anglican diocese of London, not exactly known for its support of women's theology and ministry.

We organised a series of four Friday evening meetings, one a fortnight, when a different woman would lead or facilitate the evening on a particular topic. By the time we planned the following six meetings, five out of the six were led by women who had come to one or more of the first four Friday evenings. The aim of Womenspace is 'to offer women opportunities to gather around issues of religion and spirituality'. We have always understood spirituality in the broadest sense, so that topics have included preaching, saying 'no', spiritual direction, sin, our attitudes to money and food, prayer, post-modernism, the family, and women missionaries.

When we began we sent out a flier with the Women In Theology mailing and passed word around our friends. We have never advertised widely, not least because there were very often as many women present as filled the room. Since Womenspace started, well over three hundred women have attended one or more of its evening meetings.

Those who come to Womenspace come from a wide range of religious backgrounds. Most, but not all, relate or have related in some way to Christianity. Some who come are much involved in local churches or work for a national church organisation; others are members of a denomination but feel alienated from and angry with their church; others still regard themselves as Christian but have consciously left the church; others are post-Christian or have never formally regarded themselves as Christian. Increasingly there are a number of women who come to Womenspace as serious and committed spiritual seekers but who find no home in any organised religion.

We have always insisted that Womenspace is not a group.

To the question 'How can I join the group?', the answer is always 'Just come along'. There is no advance booking (we do charge to cover costs but never knowingly stop anyone coming if they cannot pay); there is no expectation that anyone will come again. Some of the women who come to Womenspace come regularly and often, some come a couple of times each 'term' (we organise about six Womenspace evenings in the autumn, six in the winter/spring, and six in the summer), and some come perhaps two or three times a year when they are visiting London or when they are particularly interested in an evening's topic. Quite a lot of women who come travel some distance to do so.

This lack of asked-for ongoing commitment has been important to many of the women who come, and is probably more highly valued in a big city than somewhere where lives are generally less rushed. Womenspace is something you can drop in and out of, or you can come every time. The interesting thing is that no one has ever commented on the existence of an 'in' group and it is something we have never been aware of. Those who come to any one evening represent the Womenspace group for that evening. Many women, however, have met each other and become friends through Womenspace and it does offer an informal network through which women support and resource each other.

One of the richest characteristics of the group on any one Friday evening is its diversity, and it grows more diverse as the months go by. There remains a broadly Christian focus and language, but there are many different starting-points and present places on the spiritual journey. It is always (and we cannot think of *any* exception) a tolerant gathering; the message is clearly that any woman's spiritual quest and questioning is to be respected. That does not mean we tiptoe around, frightened of offending each other; there is also often quite tough questioning and debating, and we do have to be careful whom we invite to lead an evening if it is someone who has not been to Womenspace. One of the evenings which moved us most was a discussion on priesthood, which was led by one of the Anglican deacons about to be ordained to the priesthood. The gathered group included Quakers, those who had completely rejected the church, other full-time church workers, religious sisters, and Anglican lay women who had campaigned for women's ordination but who now felt cast aside without a role by the ordained women. Feelings were strong and the gulfs to communicate across huge. It was a difficult discussion, but it was honest and tough, and began, we hope, a conversation that will continue.

Women-church, and Christian women's groups and networks generally, are sometimes described as ghettos, places where like-minded 'victims' gather to share stories of oppression. Such groups, it is claimed, may offer support but they are never going to change the church or make an impact on any other social institution. That is to misunderstand (not to say display ignorance of) women-church groups. At Womenspace we do indeed share our horror stories, and look for support and encouragement from one another. Nevertheless, the 'space' is primarily a place in which 'to get on with it' – whether the 'it' is doing theology, more broadly exploring meaning in everyday experiences, or just being with God in this place with these people. Whatever the case, the experience is empowering: women who have been abused in the name of religion learn they are not alone; women who thought all theology happened in university departments discover a theological voice and language of their own.

So, individuals are changed, and change spreads. One of the most significant factors about Womenspace is the variety of religious backgrounds of participants. A liminal place is, as we have said already, a place on the boundary and as such provides a meeting place for those from different sides of the boundary: in church, out of church; Catholic, Quaker; Christian, post-Christian; Buddhist, unattached seeker. Not only do we enrich each other by the different perspectives we bring, but we take that enrichment with us when we return to our worship, work or home situations.

Websters

One of the central arguments of this book is that boundary situations are ambivalent: they offer potential for creativity, and they threaten disintegration. To remain securely and creatively on the boundary, in the gap, we need to be contained. Those of us who live semi-permanently on the church's threshold look to women-church for that sense of containment. Much has been written and said about the importance of the group – *belonging* to a community or a network of women with whom we can identify. The group provides the containment; it helps us feel 'held' in our leavings, our explorations, our desire and attempts to create something new.

On the other hand, little has been written or said about the possibilities of physical place similarly providing containment. (Rosemary Ruether's women-church plan is, of course, the notable exception.[5]) In other areas of life most of us have probably experienced what this means. Being thankful, for example, that we were ill *in our own home*, rather than when we were away. Or, if we are very ill, thankful for the security and routine of the hospital (though that is perhaps to deny present-day NHS reality). If we are an artist, we may be aware of the containing value of our studio. Walls can be imprisoning, but they can also free us to be that bit more vulnerable and chaotic, a vulnerability and chaos which gives us the chance to make something new.

It was with beliefs like these that we spent two years planning, consulting and fundraising to try to establish some sort of permanent and autonomous base for women wanting to explore the meaning of religion and spirituality in their lives. Through one of their members who came to Womenspace, we had met a small Roman Catholic community of women who also wanted to work towards a similar centre. Two members of the Vocation Sisters, Hilary Thompson and Marian Short, worked with us to see whether we could make the dream a reality.

After about two-and-a-half years of planning, building

alterations and fundraising, Websters – described as 'a meeting place and spirituality resource centre for women' – opened in October 1993 and was staffed from the end of the same year. The place itself is a former flat which began life as part of a warehouse and, if ever lived in, was empty for several years before Websters bought it and had it completely refurbished. The space gives us a large meeting room (in which on several occasions we have had at least forty women for Womenspace), an office, a cloakroom, and an open-plan 'flop space' which includes a small kitchen area, book stall, and the beginnings of a small library. The building is in Central London, about thirty yards from the hustle and bustle of Tottenham Court Road. Despite that, it has an extraordinarily peaceful feel to it – perhaps because it is at first-floor level with access over a flat roof (the lack of disabled access is our greatest regret about the property and one of the many compromises we have had to make along the way).

Websters is a registered charity and a company limited by guarantee and as such owns the property. We raised the capital to buy 6A Midford Place mostly from Roman Catholic women's communities, many of whom we knew had made a commitment to work with and for the women's movement. We then secured a considerable grant over three years towards our salary costs from one of the large Quaker trusts. Without the generosity and vision of these bodies, as well as a large number of individuals, Websters would never have got off the ground. Needless to say, we are not yet anything like secure in our funding. Indeed, as this book nears publication the future of the project is in the balance. Part of the struggle is financial, part is the hard task of working with the very diversity Websters seeks to affirm.

The hope of Websters' founders was to provide opportunities for a wide diversity of women to meet like-minded others and also women of different backgrounds from themselves. Websters, the meeting-place, is an attempt to set up a loom. The weavers are the women who meet there, criss-crossing the boundaries of their lives and ideas and religious aspirations, enriching each other and the religious and other communities from which they come, which so much need the warmth and energy of such exchanges.

9

A Rite to Leave

The Jungian analyst Bani Shorter tells the story of Nicole, a musician, who found herself in a situation of crisis over her marriage and her music. The marriage ended, and her husband remained in the house, the home they had made together. A decisive moment in her coming to terms with her situation as a grown woman was an occasion when, her former husband being away, she went back alone to what had been their joint home. She later reported to Bani Shorter what had happened.

It had taken her three days to complete what she had set out to do. She had cleaned the place from top to bottom. She had mowed the lawn, pruned the hedge and weeded the garden. She had forced herself to do these things, she said. She had cried a lot, but she had forced herself to sleep in the house alone each night, as well.

When her task had been completed at last, on the evening of the third day, she had gone out and gathered flowers from the garden, brought them in and arranged them in all her favourite places. The house was beautiful, she said. She had then bathed and dressed and packed her bag. But, before she had left, during the long twilight of the still evening, she had drawn her instrument from the case, lifted her fingers and played a recital of her favourite pieces. When she closed the door at last, she put her key through the letter-box, leaving the home-no-longer-hers behind, she felt, for ever.[1]

This story illustrates the power of ritual to help us face the small deaths in our lives and move forward through important changes. In this instance, says Bani Shorter, Nicole had 'conducted a funeral rite for the death of a romantic childhood fantasy and, in so doing, had reached a new stage of life'.

This was a very personal ritual, concerned with an individual's experience of loss. But ritual is more often and more usually a social affair; indeed, much of its power lies in the public nature of its proclamation and the shared story it enacts. An example of this sort of ritual arose after a tragedy in Scarborough and was later recounted in *The Guardian* (4th August 1993).

In the summer of 1993, the Holbeck Hotel in Scarborough was destroyed by a mudslide when the cliff it was built on collapsed. Its destruction meant a real sense of loss to the local community, who had known it not only as a landmark but as a place filled with memories of wedding receptions, retirement parties, birthday treats, and other special family gatherings. Now it had gone, and its remains were being visited by sightseers and inspected by surveyors anxious about further subsidence. A woman who had lived opposite the hotel for thirteen years expressed feelings both of loss and of being 'thrown' by the ensuing chaos: 'It's been like losing a friend, but life since has been anything but normal. More like a cross between living in a safari-park and a prisoner-of-war camp. It will be good to get back to some sort of reality.'

The vicar of the local parish organised a memorial service, during which former staff from the hotel took part in a procession down the aisle, carrying cutlery, visitors' registers, and tiles salvaged from the Edwardian mansion. The vicar wrote a hymn for the occasion, 'A Litany of Sorrow', and described the aim of the service as being to resolve some of the conflicting feelings about the hotel's sudden and dramatic destruction.

Ritual is essentially a language – a language of demonstration. In ritual, we act out with our bodies and find that we can say more than is in our minds. When our thoughts cannot move us forward, ritual often can. It can make statements about time, about what is past, present and future. And it can define space:

> Ritual can help us create boundaries. To create sacred space is an act of protection. Ritual can create a 'liberated zone' of the spirit, can change an atmosphere, make a space ours. It can become a political act: the Women's Peace Camp at Greenham Common can be seen as an ongoing ritual, reclaiming the space of the missile base for peace. Marches and demonstrations may also be rituals of this sort.[2]

This quotation from Starhawk is a reminder that ritual is not primarily introspective, for an individual or a group. Ritual, like many other aspects of religion, has been distorted by the privatising trend ubiquitous in our society. People talk of 'doing rituals', often on their own. Whilst ritual can be an important element in our stories of change (as in the story of Nicole above), at its most powerful ritual is something we *participate in* rather than something we *do*. For, as well as being a language of demonstration, ritual is also a way we effect change because the change is made public – we have witnesses to a new order; we can *together* declare the past as past, or together acknowledge a new boundary and definition for our group.

If we are Christians, we look to the churches to provide public rituals to mark significant changes in our lives. People are baptised, confirmed, married and buried in church, often even when they have little other contact with a church. As we have already said, however, the churches are no better at dealing with loss than the rest of society. Creative services around times of loss, like the one in Scarborough for the hotel, are rare. Gerald Arbuckle, a Roman Catholic social anthropologist, makes a plea in his book, *Grieving for Change*, for a spirituality of grieving. This means first acknowledging that there is a real loss and therefore something to grieve *for*. Among the case studies he uses, he quotes the words of a grieving parishioner:

> I am now in my fifties. When all the liturgical changes came in after Vatican II, I was very happy. How good it was to hear the prayers in English and to learn about how we share in the priesthood of Christ, how we must bring the Gospel of justice to a world in change! In those days I never thought about what we were giving up. In fact, the changes were sudden and we felt the old ways of doing things were wrong. Now I find myself – with so many of my friends – at times yearning for the old days when everything was clear about what we had to believe and do in the Church. I look back to the time of Father X, a saintly man, and to the Sunday evening devotions. Sometimes we all feel angry, even depressed, about all the changes. Certainly I want the parish to settle down. And so do others.[3]

The feelings of depression, anger and longing for stability expressed here are probably quite common. Arbuckle describes the parishioner as suffering from *delayed* grief. Many changes had taken place over the years since Vatican II and there had been no public ritual in the parish to help her realise and express the loss that would be part of those changes. The past has not really been let go of, hence 'yearning for the old days when everything was clear'.

In order to arrive, we must first leave.

This book has been thought about, and to some extent written, over a number of years. Its long gestation is reflected in its content and argument. In other words, it has been written by insiders – by two women who live consciously (and sometimes, it feels, acutely) on the boundary, in a place characterised by its in-betweenness.

Perhaps the greatest loss for both of us has been our taking leave of religious and monastic life. Ironically, it was probably that lifestyle which has provided us both with a training, and equipped us with some practical tools, to live liminally. We miss many things about religious life – particularly perhaps the liturgical life and the sheer security of it all – but neither of us for one moment regrets the move we each made for our own reasons. We visit the community often, usually cooking and gardening at the guest house when we stay, and we remain involved with each other's lives. The newly ordered relationships have not been won easily nor are they comfortable for everyone, but there is a sense of owning the past *as past* in a way that is true for those involved in the present relationship.

There are other times when leaving a community, of whatever kind, is much more difficult because past hurts and general relationship messes cannot be resolved. There is then nothing to do but leave with a lot of loose threads which may well have to remain loose for ever. It is much harder in this sort of circumstance to incorporate the past into the future in a way that is potentially creative for all concerned.

However, the leaving might not have to do with people at all. We may need to say goodbye to long-held beliefs or to specific images of God, or to a whole religious system. Alternatively, our loss may be more general in its feel: 'The old answers that used to speak, no longer speak to me, and the passages of scripture in which I once felt comfort are no longer comforting. There is a silence in me that as yet has no voice.'[4] The fact of the matter is that, as with other aspects of our lives, many of us are currently experiencing change and confusion in what we believe and how we express those beliefs. In and around the churches (and among the 'unchurched') there seems to be a good deal of grief, much of it unacknowledged and unexpressed. It is our belief that this represents a significant block to the emergence of still more energetic and creative theology, liturgy, and community building. We cannot create the new with real vigour until we have let go of that in the old which holds us up.

People will be at different places in the grief process. Some will know they must let go, but cannot do it yet. Others will be in the throes of mourning, having let go of things previously held dear. Others still will be on the verge of coming through grief to a place that feels like a new home. In terms of the three phases of change we looked at earlier and their parallel in the phases of a rite of passage, we suggest that many of us are needing a pre-liminal rite; that is, we need to let go *into* the wilderness, or the gap of change, not let go *of* the wilderness, tempting though the thought might be.

Just as through a simple yet powerful ritual Nicole found a way to move on in her life, and the people of Scarborough were able publicly to acknowledge the loss of all that the Holbeck Hotel meant to them, so we suggest that some short and simple ritual may help us to leave behind aspects of our religion which block rather than aid our journey of faith.

Taking leave

We offer the following simple ritual which may give rise to other ideas about how we can begin to let go of things we need to leave behind in order that the new is free to be born.

Preparation

We suggest that this ritual, and any similar ritual, should form part of an ongoing group experience. Several of you may get together specifically to look at the grief you can identify in your own story, or the ritual may arise out of an existing group where the issues of change and loss have already emerged.

- Spend an evening (or a day) together, sharing whatever each of you wants to of your story as it relates to your spiritual journey. You may agree to focus particularly on your experience of change and loss on that journey. Give each person a set amount of time – say, eight minutes – to speak without interruption of any kind. The other members of the group listen as attentively as they can. It helps to have something to pass from one person to another which is held by the speaker for the time she speaks. This can be a stick, a pebble, a ball of wool, even a juggling ball – anything that is easy and comfortable to hold.

- When you have each had a chance to speak, take a break.

- The second part of the evening (or day) is the simple ritual itself. We came across the following ritual, originally created by Gerard Whiteford SM, in Gerald Arbuckle's book *Refounding the Church* (p. 198). We reproduce it here as something obviously tried and tested, recognising that different groups will want to revise it to make it their own. In particular, a fairly orthodox Christianity is assumed, but this need not be so: different readings and a 'candle of life', say, rather than a paschal candle would make the ritual more accessible to those unsure of or alienated by clearly Christian symbols.

Preliminary instructions
- As participants enter in silence into the darkened room they are given lighted candles and move into groups of eight (or fewer) in circles; the paschal candle is alight in the centre of the room; meditative background music can be played.

- It is advisable not to extend the ritual beyond approximately one hour.

Process
1. *Leader:* Reads Isaiah 45:7. Invites all to enter into the darkness of the tomb so that they may discover the newness of the resurrection.

2. *Reader:* Reads Psalm 143.

3. *Leader:* Invites all to ponder the question 'What significant thing do I feel I have lost personally or communally?'

Pause for a few moments.

Invites participants to name some loss or grief that they have experienced, advising them to keep their naming to one word or a phrase. There is no discussion on what is named. After each participant names a loss, then she/he extinguishes their candle; the paschal candle and lights are extinguished by the leader.

4. *Reader:* Once all have extinguished their candles, Psalm 88 is read. Silence for a lengthy period.

5. *Leader:* Invites participants to identify some newness or joy that has entered the group or their ministry; the paschal candle is lit. After a short time the leader invites them to name the newness in the group (or write it on sheets around the room). Each participant, having named a newness, then lights his/her candle from the paschal candle.

6. *Leader:* After all candles have been lit, there is a short period of silence, followed by the leader reading Revelation 21:1–7. A resurrection hymn follows. All are then invited to give the sign of peace.

10
Meaning, Community, Integrity

We have dwelt at length on the liminal experience we ourselves know most about; but liminality is not just about the
place where feminist Christians find themselves. This book
speaks primarily to all those who experience themselves as
or can recognise themselves as in some sense boundary-
dwellers. The range is wide. There are many ways of
experiencing the images used in this book and they can
sometimes seem mutually exclusive, even to those on similar
paths: we ourselves speak from an Anglican stance; our dissi-
dent-Roman Catholic friends, boundary-dwellers in their
own church, sometimes startle us with attitudes that seem
to us as Roman as the Pope. To a Methodist friend we
ourselves seem to create too Anglican an atmosphere: in
spite of our intentions, we have given her the feeling of being
outside our boundaries. Some Christians, again, are anxious
for the whole church to see itself in more practical ways as
on the boundary – or beyond it – in terms of identifying
with the poor, the outcasts of society. These are all cross-
currents, forbidding the adoption of one neat map or path.

Those who wish to bring their professional skills (for
example, as sociologist or ethicist) to the service of the
Christian community often discover that this means they
can meet that community only where it is as it were venturing
beyond itself. This may be professionally and personally

demanding and often disappointing, but usually falls short of the more painful experience of persons or groups of other than the prevailing race or sexual orientation.

Meaning

The struggle for meaning may well form part of the experience of liminality: the liminal situation, in turn, provides a sense of movement and hence of purpose and of hope – though only to those who are learning to find the meaning of their lives as a process, if not necessarily a progress. Everything in the natural world speaks of movement – of coming to be, growing, aging, dying, re-emerging in new generations or in renewed life. Wilderness – time of transition and change – is always at hand. Many draw back from it, especially, it seems, in the context of religious experience; or at best they find interest only in a private journey of their own, either through 'the world my wilderness' or through some crisis in their faith.

We do not want to undervalue personal individual choice and experience, but we do want to affirm strongly the common human elements in such experience and, in that awareness, the responsibility to accept involvement with others who are on the same path as ourselves.

Margaret Thatcher's claim (no society, only individuals) may leave even many conservative people looking sheepish and apologetic, but she only expressed the way many people – perhaps most – feel and behave, that is, with little sense of belonging to some greater whole, or of the responsibility that goes with this. A sense of community is not easy to discover, still less maintain, in a society that puts competition ahead of co-operation, getting your money's worth (dignified as 'value for money') ahead of service. Moreover, those of us who do aspire to co-operate and to serve are apt to flounder about in a world where such behaviour seems as old hat as most religious notions.

The traditional language of Christian belief and practice is not now widely known or understood in the UK (witness the recent misreporting of proponents of 'modern' music in an Anglo-Catholic church in Oxford as being 'evangelicals'); practising Christian believers are fewer, and their Christian identity sets them increasingly far apart from the average everyday life of the nation; against this, however, it must be said that there are equally important gaps in communication between the intellectual extremes among believers. Like the national media, many Christians tend to go for simple, primary-coloured, largely unexamined formularies.

Community

We have tended when talking about liminality in previous chapters to focus on its ambivalent and in-between characteristics. But van Gennep, and the Turners after him, emphasise another central feature of the liminal experience, that of *communitas*, that is, close-knit, spontaneous, non-hierarchical community. So, for example, in the Turners' study of medieval pilgrimage as a liminoid phenomenon, they note the *communitas* which springs up among the pilgrims.[1] Package holidays can create something similar. When we are temporarily away from home, out of our usual roles, we are more free in our relationships, and if we are somewhere 'strange' we are likely to make some unusual friends who are sharing a similar experience.

This is a reminder to us of the value of community in providing us with a sense of belonging and boundary in a place of transition. Such communities (like most communities, in fact) are generally made up of people who are thrown together, rather than those who have carefully selected each other.

And so with the bit of the wilderness in which we find ourselves: we discover our fellow boundary-dwellers. It does not matter in the end whether we regard ourselves as having been called together by God or thrown together by circumstance: the task is to make community and to learn how to relate to other communities. Perhaps the making of community is a particular task for boundary-dwellers, because they live at the place of meeting. There we must learn to meet not only with one another, but with those who enter the place of boundary from different directions.

To talk of spontaneous community is not to suggest that it is an instantly perfect community – no community is. Like any community, it must be nurtured and struggled with. Its lack of structure will probably make community-building harder, not easier. Like all communities, it will make demands on those who belong to it. It will have its own discipline, and require responsibility and accountability in its members. Words like 'discipline', 'responsibility' and 'accountability' are not often associated with those whom the churches regard as 'fringers'. Nor are they a common part of the language of those who regard themselves as marginalised victims. But in our experience, the stronger and more self-confident the individual or group beginning to define themselves in terms of threshold rather than margin, the more conscious they will be of the need for committed community-building.

Integrity

We see integrity as a quality of those who speak and (more important) live out what they believe to be true, a task never more difficult than for those who find themselves challenging their fellows, when it seems easier to keep quiet, to be private and personal and let the world go by. And those who have any sort of vision are a challenge not just to their fellow humans but to themselves. We may feel, rightly enough, that we know something of the challenge that Jesus offered to his own generation; we do not have the sort of information needed to know the challenge Jesus himself had to meet. In the religious terms of his day, the gospel story of his forty days in the wilderness gives some notion of his struggle for integrity, and we have seen also how that struggle persisted through his public ministry and reached a climax in the events leading to his death.

For many Christian women the challenge to wholeness

means that they must venture out into a place where the dualistic attitudes that have always tended to afflict Christianity can be broken down. The acceptance of women as ordained ministers in the churches breaks through ancient barriers not least of fear by men *and* women of women's bodily nature and sexuality. But these fears are (it is obvious) not ended by church legislation. At best such legislation can provide a context of legality within a church setting where new attitudes may slowly be learned. About homosexuality, perhaps only the Society of Friends offers the vantage point of some formal acceptance of a wider range of natural behaviour than other larger and older Christian churches can yet contemplate. As far as race is concerned, the churches may think that they have the theory right at last, but the depth of racism in most white people is still greater than most of us are able to acknowledge. Theological integrity is as exacting as any: though the greatest of Christian teachers have never doubted that we ought to be modest and humble in what we venture to say about God, church leaders are nervous in their response to attempts to modify long-held popular views, and the Anthony Freemans of the Church of England (for instance) have to learn how to leave behind the traditional security of the incumbent and accept and make the most of a liminal position.

So we have tried in this book to make two things clear. First, those who believe themselves to be driven into the wilderness by the Spirit of God, just as Jesus was, need to recognise that they are being driven forward, not out – forward over the barriers that seek to limit and constrain the Spirit's activity. As long as the churches are alive, there are always groups of Christians subject to this divine pressure, for a variety of reasons (beware of those who think their cause is the only one). Some feel fairly sure of a lifetime in this wilderness for themselves and for the movement of which they are a part – to draw water from the well of hope a very long rope is needed – but the movement is still forward, not out. There are groups who see themselves as 'holding the fort': it is hardly possible for their critics to see them as forward-moving. Some are very firm about severing the links that bind them to their Christian past, but it is a past that they still carry with them.

Secondly, those of us who feel ourselves to be driven beyond the limits of the churches' or society's comfort, need to go beyond our own individual experience in order to make community (not just common cause, which can produce nothing better than a ghetto) with others on the same path. We not only need the loyalty and accountability that community membership entails; we also need to be able to face together the church community that reared us, and say: 'It is from the very resources that you have given us that we now ask you these questions.'

Finally, in the context of the struggle for meaning, for community and for integrity, two things keep recurring in conversations with other women and in our own lives. They are the values of silence and of not knowing. They are, of course, intimately related.

Hannah remembers being in conversation with someone some years ago when, in answer to a question, she heard herself say, 'I don't know'. She cannot remember what the question was – it's irrelevant – but the quality of the answer took her aback. It was as if she had just heard herself speak some great truth. Indeed, it probably was the truest thing she could say to herself at the time. It was, paradoxically, full of knowledge. Hannah had not thought about it for some time until very recently during a Womenspace evening of story-telling she heard a number of the women present, in the course of telling their own stories, say, in one way or another, 'I don't know'.

It is hard when we are campaigning for women's ordination, for inclusive language in the liturgy, for a university chair in feminist theology, or whatever, to be able to *know* forcefully and not know at the same time. If you are a Christian feminist, you will be battling somewhere, over something, with someone. The same applies to any other sort of boundary-dweller. It is important for us to know what is our experience, to know that it matters, and to know how to voice it. But it is also vital – literally life-giving – for us to find some deep breathing space in which to hear ourselves say 'I don't know'. It is part of the essence of journeying and at the heart of the pivotal moment of change.

As for silence, even 'poor, noisy, talkative Christianity' has plenty to say about silence. Yet one of the saddest limitations of some Christians is that they know silence only as failure, cowardice, or a dangerous laying open of the person to invasive evil. At the best there is little or no space allowed between 'Be still, and know that I am God' and 'Here am I: send me'. But silence is an irreplaceable element, the sun and rain of human life and growth, the deep breathing space mentioned above. To be sure, silence can indeed threaten disintegration: words are containers and shapers. They have an ambivalence familiar in this book, a quality that is both creative and limiting. To explore the thresholds of our faith experience, we need to let go into silence – which is itself both creative and dangerous. We need some point of focus – the silent circle, the safe space – for silence is a very intimate experience not to be entered into lightly. A 'shared silence' can be deadening and deadly where the participants are resolutely private, 'keeping themselves to themselves'. But, positively, silence can be a way of venturing on to the thresholds of faith and of meaning: in silence you can share and express something together with those who cannot share the same words. You can express what you know and explore beyond that frontier. Silence is the language of not-knowing. It is also the ground in which both love and knowledge can grow and flourish.

Epilogue:

'With love to the church'[1]

Rosemary Ruether has suggested that Christian feminists might think of spending nine-tenths of their time, energy and resources working at new ways of being church – getting on with their own theology, creating new liturgies, and so on. The other one-tenth of time, energy and resources could be offered by them to the institutional church, working and arguing more directly with its leaders, structures and committees. This epilogue is offered as our tithe in this book. Because we are both Anglicans, we speak first to the Church of England, but hope also to offer to the historic churches generally a few questions and reflections raised by boundary-dwellers who attempt to live as honestly as they can in the gap between what has been and what might be.

These brief reflections are offered under headings of different aspects of the church's mission.

EDUCATION

- Where do our education programmes take place, both lay and ordained? We need to pay careful attention to the *context* of learning, since physical space can provide an invaluable 'container' for open and risky exploration.

- Are we prepared to educate people *out of* and *away from*, as well as *into*?

123

- How can the churches support and encourage centres of learning which are religiously pluralistic and 'open' in their assumptions and base-lines?

PASTORAL CARE

- Do churches have any pastoral responsibility for those who dwell on their boundaries? To regard them as 'problems', 'fringers' or 'the needy' is to deny them their humanity and religious integrity. Are the churches' official pastors prepared to receive pastoral care from the boundary-dwellers? Can the institutional churches address the issues of power in this and other pastoral situations?

MISSION

- We are in the Decade of Evangelism/Evangelisation. How are the churches using their boundaries and boundary-dwellers as places and people of *meeting*?

- Do we want people to have faith, or to have faith within a particular (i.e. Christian) framework? If the latter, is this a worthwhile priority and project for the end of the twentieth century?

- In their encouragement of inter-faith dialogue, how can the churches hear the fruits of that dialogue other than from those who are within the 'mainstream' of their own tradition? If *the* place of meeting and dialogue is the boundary, how does the church engage in dialogue with the boundary communities?

WORSHIP

- Much contemporary worship fails to connect with people's experience. It is frequently boring and irrelevant to most of those not actively playing a part in the proceedings. Most church liturgy cannot be said to be a ritual expression of the community's life. Can clergy hand over the creation of liturgy to those whose lives it is supposed to express before God, recognising that they too will be a part of the group? It is not enough that some chosen members of the congregation are given parts in what is still essentially the vicar's play.

- How can congregations be helped to listen to their own stories in such a way as enables them to create such liturgy? Isn't this an important priestly role?

- The stories we have listened to indicate the need, for some of us at least, for a good deal of silence within worship, and for space in which we can 'not know'. Silence and symbolic gesture are two important ingredients in any ritual concerned with change.

ECCLESIOLOGY

- The church, as Ruether points out, is the historic institution *and* the spirit-filled community in dialectical relationship with each other — or, to be more precise, historic institutions and spirit-filled communities. For we are talking about a lot of very diverse Christian communities which contain a lot of very diverse Christians and some who would only tentatively (if at all) describe themselves as 'Christian'. Womenspace, for example, we would want to claim as trying to create spirit-filled community, but not all who come would define 'spirit' in Christian terms; it is a community of faith, rather than a community of a particular faith, even though Christians are in the vast majority.

- Accepting this rich diversity, what is the church's understanding of itself? How can it sustain creative and defining boundaries without stunting its own growth and ability to respond to newly discovered truth?

- How can the diverse communities foster creative communication between each other? The Council of Churches for Britain and Ireland, for example, does not reflect the real diversity of the Christian Church in Britain and Ireland — only the historic, institutional forms.

FINANCE

- The church, it is said, is the only organisation which exists for those who are not its members.[2] Money has a powerful way of telling the truth. So, how far is this popular saying about the church reflected in the churches' financial priorities?

- In the forced financial reorganisation currently facing the Church of England (and doubtless other churches too), will diverse forms of 'belonging' to the church, different worship needs, and a concern to meet and communicate with those outside the churches, be reflected in the new spending patterns?

MONASTICISM

- To return briefly to what Endress has to say about monasticism,[3] we must ask: Is the monastic person liminal because she or he is living a life *separated* from 'normal society'? 'The monk,' says Endress, traditionally 'wavers, so to speak, between two worlds – the world of the sacred and the world of the profane – without being a part of either' (p. 148). Yet in a rite of passage the liminal person is neither one thing nor another *and* both; that is liminality's central ambiguity. Boundaries separate one thing from another *and* they provide the meeting place for both. A contemplative life, wherever and however it is lived, surely proclaims the meeting of heaven and earth, the sacred and the profane, and in so doing denies that they are separate.
  Might not a monastic lifestyle have much to say to us, not so much about separation, as about the relationship between limitation and potentiality?

Appendix

A wilderness liturgy organised by the Southwark Women Seeking Ordination Group, Petertide, and held outside Southwark Cathedral during the ordination service, 3rd July 1983.

> She who would valiant be
> 'Gainst all disaster
> Let her in constancy
>   Follow the Master.
> There's no discouragement
> Shall make her once relent
> Her first avowed intent
> To be a pilgrim.
>
> Who so beset her round
> With dismal stories,
> Do but themselves confound –
>   Her strength the more is.
> No foes shall stay her might
> Though she with giants fight!
> She will make good her right
> To be a pilgrim.

Since, Lord, thou dost defend
Us with thy Spirit,
We know we at the end
    Shall life inherit.
Then fancies flee away!
I'll fear not what men say,
I'll labour night and day
To be a pilgrim.
                    (John Bunyan, altered)

Old Testament Reading: Exodus 19:2–6

Hymn: Tell out my soul, the greatness of the Lord

New Testament Reading: 1 Peter 2:4–10

Sermon

Intercessions
O Living God, we pray for your holy people, the Church.
We ask that every member may be freed to serve you in
truth and grace.
We remember our foremothers. We remember all women
who have recognised that to be a person of faith is to respond
in action. We give thanks:
For Miriam, poetess of the Exodus, leader through the wil-
derness;
For Deborah, a mother and a judge in Israel;
For Rachel, traveller with Jacob;
For the woman who bathed Jesus' feet with her tears;
For Mary Magdalene, first apostle of the resurrection.
We give you thanks, O God.

Let us remember all those women who have faced the
unknown in faith and met fear with courage. We give thanks:
For all those women who have dared to step forward and
lead;

For all those women who have challenged the stereotypes of society and risked standing alone.

We give you thanks, O God.

Let us remember women who have struggled to reform our history, who have sought in their time to minister to the needs of the hurt, the disadvantaged and the alienated in our land. We give thanks:
For Florence Nightingale, Elizabeth Fry, the Pankhursts, Josephine Butler and, above all, for all those without a name.

We give you thanks, O God.

We pray for those, known and unknown, who have laboured in the struggle before us. We give thanks:
For Maude Royden, Phoebe Willetts, Mollie Batten, Elsie Chamberlain, Una Kroll, Reverend Florence Li Tim Oi.

We give you thanks, O God.

O holy and sustaining God, make us worthy to inherit their valour and vision. Challenge us again lest we wither and perish by holding to the familiar when it has lost its savour. As your daughters and sons, may we be brought nearer to a new vision of your love, through the grace of the Holy Spirit. Amen.

The wilderness meal

The Israelites complained to Moses and Aaron in the wilderness and said, 'If only we had died at Yahweh's hand in Egypt, where we sat round the fleshpots and had plenty of bread to eat! But you have brought us out into this wilderness to let this whole assembly starve to death!'
   Moses and Aaron then said to all the Israelites, 'In the evening you will know that it was Yahweh who brought you out of Egypt, and in the morning you will see the glory of Yahweh, because he has heeded your complaints against

him; it is not against us that you bring your complaints; we are nothing.'

That evening a flock of quails flew in and settled all over the camp, and in the morning a fall of dew lay all around it. When the dew was gone, there in the wilderness, fine flakes appeared as hoar frost on the ground. Moses said to them, 'That is the bread which Yahweh has given you to eat.'

The honey cake is handed round.

Israel called the food manna; it was white, like coriander seed, and it tasted like a wafer made with honey.

'This,' said Moses, 'is the command which Yahweh has given: Take a full omer of it to be kept for future generations, so that they may see the bread with which I fed you in the wilderness when I brought you out of Egypt.'

The Israelites ate the manna for forty years until they came to a land where they could settle; they ate it until they came to the frontier of the land of Canaan.

Reading from Isaiah 66:5–13

Hear the word of Yahweh, you who revere his word: Your fellow countrymen who hate you, who spurn you because you bear my name, have said, 'Let Yahweh show his glory, then we shall see you rejoice'; but they shall be put to shame. That roar from the city, that uproar in the temple, is the sound of Yahweh's dealing retribution to his foes.

Shall a woman bear a child without pains? Give birth to a son before the onset of labour? Who has heard of anything like this? Who has seen any such thing? Shall a country be born after one day's labour, shall a nation to brought to birth all in a moment? But Zion, at the onset of her pangs, bore her children. Shall I bring to the point of birth and not deliver? Yahweh says: Shall I who deliver close the womb? Your God has spoken.

The milk is passed round.

Rejoice with Jerusalem and exult in her, all you who love her; share her joy with all your heart, all you who mourn over her. Then you may suck and be fed from her breasts that give comfort, delighting in her plentiful milk. For thus says Yahweh: 'I will send peace flowing over her like a river, and the wealth of nations like a stream in flood; she shall suckle you and you shall be carried in her arms and dandled on her knees. As a mother comforts her child, so will I myself comfort you, and you shall find comfort in Jerusalem.'

Hymn: Come, thou holy Paraclete

The covenant between us – from Ruth 1:16–18

'Where you go, I will go, and where you stay, I will stay.
Your people shall be my people, and your God my God.
Where you die, I will die, and there I will be buried.
I swear a solemn oath before Yahweh your God: nothing but death shall divide us.'

We offer the sign of peace.

References

Introduction

1. Bani Shorter, *Border People*, Guild Lecture No. 211 (The Guild of Pastoral Psychology, 1982), p.7.

Chapter 1

1. This chapter, and others, contains material originally published as an article by Hannah Ward, 'Boundary-dwellers' in *The Way* (April 1993).
2. G. Caplan, *An Approach to Community Mental Health* and *Principles of Preventative Psychiatry* (both Tavistock, 1964).
3. Michael Hobbs in a useful article reviewing work on crisis theory, 'Crisis intervention in theory and practice: a selective review' in *British Journal of Medical Psychiatry*, 57 (1984), pp.23–4.
4. Caplan, *An Approach to Community Mental Health*, op. cit.
5. G. Arbuckle, *Grieving for Change* (Geoffrey Chapman, 1991), p.49; and see *The Dominion*, 26th October 1989 (New Zealand), p.1.
6. C. S. Lewis (originally attributed to N. W. Clerk), *A Grief Observed* (Faber & Faber, 1961), p.29.
7. G. Arbuckle, *Refounding the Church* (Geoffrey Chapman, 1993), p.183.
8. Roger Grainger, *Change to Life* (Darton, Longman & Todd, 1993), p.48.
9. P. Ricoeur, *The Conflict of Interpretations: Essays in Hermeneutics* (Evanston, USA: Northwestern University Press, 1974).

132

10. Arbuckle, *Grieving for Change*, op. cit., p.68. See also Walter Brueggeman, *Praying the Psalms* (Winona, Minnesota, USA: St Mary's Press, 1989) for a fascinating study of the Psalms based on the categories of orientation, disorientation and reorientation.
11. There is, however, just such a retirement service in Grainger, *Change to Life*, op. cit., pp.150–53.
12. Arbuckle, *Grieving for Change*, op. cit., p.68.
13. Sogyal Rinpoche, 'The Survival of Consciousness: a Tibetan Buddhist Perspective'. As far as we know this is an unpublished paper. See also Sogyal Rinpoche, *The Tibetan Book of Living and Dying* (Rider Books, 1992).

Chapter 2

1. A. van Gennep, *The Rites of Passage*, translated by M. B. Vizedom and G. L. Caffee (Routledge & Kegan Paul, 1960).
2. See especially Victor W. Turner, *The Ritual Process* (Pelican Books, 1974), and Victor Turner and Edith Turner, *Image and Pilgrimage in Christian Culture: Anthropological Perspectives* (Basil Blackwell, 1978).
3. Richard Endress, 'The Monastery as a Liminal Community' in *American Benedictine Review*, Vol. 26 (June 1975).
4. Mary Douglas, *Purity and Danger* (Routledge & Kegan Paul, 1978), p.2.
5. Ibid., p.94.
6. Ibid., p.95.
7. Kenneth Leech, 'Not Survival but Prophecy' in *Encounter and Exchange*, No. 18 (Spring 1977).
8. Endress, op. cit., pp.149–50.

Chapter 3

1. Harry Williams, *The True Wilderness* (Constable, 1965).
2. Carlo Carretto, *Letters from the Desert* (Darton, Longman & Todd, 1974), *In Search of the Beyond* (Darton, Longman & Todd, 1975), *The God who Comes* (Darton, Longman & Todd, 1974).
3. The same Greek word is variously translated as wilderness, desert or (adjectivally) lonely place.
4. Carretto, *Letters from the Desert*, p.11.
5. Ibid., p.73.
6. G. Gutierrez, *A Theology of Liberation* (Orbis Books, 1973), p.157.

7. Tissa Balasuriya, *Planetary Theology* (SCM, 1984), p.158.
8. A detailed account of this sorry tale can be found in Malcolm Johnson, *Outside the Gate: St Botolphs, Aldgate, 950–1944* (Stepney Books, 1994).

Chapter 4

1. Marie-Eloise Rosenblatt in *The Way* (January 1990), p. 10.
2. These terms are used instead of 'Old' and 'New' Testaments as a more equitable way of describing the origins of these two parts of the Bible of Christians.
3. Robert Alter, *The World of Biblical Literature* (SPCK, 1992), p.51.
4. See in particular Ulric Mauser, *Christ in the Wilderness*, Studies in Biblical Theology No. 39 (SCM Press, 1952).
5. See, for example, Phyllis Trible, *Texts of Terror* (Fortress Press, 1984), p.9.
6. J. B. Lightfoot, *Galatians* (Macmillan, 1865), pp.87–90 (in 1902 edition).
7. *Benedictine Thesaurus* (Rome, 1977).
8. From an ancient homily for Holy Saturday.
9. Caroline Glyn, 'The Sleepers' in *In Him Was Life* (Gollancz, 1975).

Chapter 5

1. Andrew Louth, *The Wilderness of God* (Darton, Longman & Todd, 1991).
2. The words are from the hymn 'For ever with the Lord!', by J. Montgomery (1835).
3. Charles Williams (ed.), *The Letters of Evelyn Underhill* (Longmans, Green and Co., 1943), Introduction, p.13.
4. Ibid., Introduction, pp.14, 15.
5. 'In torment and effort to serve the brethren'.
6. *Abba* (Longmans, Green and Co., 1940), pp.73ff.
7. Quoted in Anne Ridler's Introduction (p.xxx) to Charles Williams, *The Image of the City and Other Essays* (Oxford University Press, 1958).
8. C. S. Lewis, *The Great Divorce* (Geoffrey Bles, 1946).
9. A. N. Wilson, *C. S. Lewis: A Biography* (Collins, 1990), p.283.
10. N. W. Clerk (C. S. Lewis), *A Grief Observed* (Faber & Faber, 1961, 1964), p.11.
11. Dorothy L. Sayers, *The Mind of the Maker* (Methuen, 1941).
12. Charles Williams, *All Hallows Eve* (Faber & Faber, 1945).

13. Edwin Muir, *An Autobiography* (The Hogarth Press, 1954). Quotations are from the 1987 edition.
14. *Variations on a Time Theme* VI in Edwin Muir, *Collected Poems* (Faber & Faber, 1963), 1984 edition, pp.45–7.
15. From 'The Breaking' in *Collected Poems*, 1984 edition, p.305.

Chapter 6

1. Information about Women In Theology, Catholic Women's Network, Womenspace and Websters can be obtained from Websters, 6A Midford Place, Tottenham Court Road, London W1P 9HH (please enclose s.a.e.), tel. 071 388 0026.
2. Janet Morley and Hannah Ward (eds), *Celebrating Women* (Women In Theology/Movement for the Ordination of Women, 1986); new and greatly expanded edition, Hannah Ward, Jennifer Wild, Janet Morley (eds), due to be published by SPCK, Easter 1995.
3. The St Hilda Community, *Women Included* (SPCK, 1992).
4. See Jim Cotter, *Prayer at Night* (Cairns Publications, 1983).
5. *Daily Mail*, 22nd July 1991.
6. Joanna Macy, *Despair and Personal Power in the Nuclear Age* (New Society Publishers, 1983).

Chapter 7

1. Mary Daly, *Outercourse: The Be-Dazzling Voyage* (The Women's Press, 1993), p.46.
2. A sermon preached to St Matthew's, Brixton, Pentecost 11, 3rd August 1986.
3. A contributor in Rosie Miles, *Not in Our Name: Voices of Women who have left the Church* (Southwell Board of Social Responsibility, 1994), p.49.
4. Rosemary Radford Ruether, *Women-Church: Theology and Practice of Feminist Liturgical Communities* (Harper & Row, 1985), especially Chapter 7.

Chapter 8

1. Daly, op. cit., p.46.
2. Ruether, op. cit., p.3.
3. Ibid., p.4.
4. Miles, op. cit.
5. Ruether, op. cit., pp.146–8.

Chapter 9

1. Bani Shorter, *An Image Darkly Forming: Women and Initiation* (Routledge & Kegan Paul, 1987), pp.11–12.
2. Starhawk, *Truth or Dare: Encounters with Power, Authority and Mystery* (Harper & Row, 1987), p.149.
3. Arbuckle, *Grieving for Change*, op. cit., p.12.
4. Kathleen Fischer, *Women at the Well: Feminist Perspectives on Spiritual Direction* (SPCK, 1989), p.64.

Chapter 10

1. Victor Turner and Edith Turner, *Image and Pilgrimage in Christian Culture: Anthropological Perspectives* (Basil Blackwell, 1978).

Epilogue

1. This title is taken from Monica Furlong, *With Love to the Church*.
2. The saying is attributed to William Temple.
3. See p.31 above.